EYEWITNESS VISUAL DICTIONARIES

THE VISUAL
DICTIONARY *of*
BUILDINGS

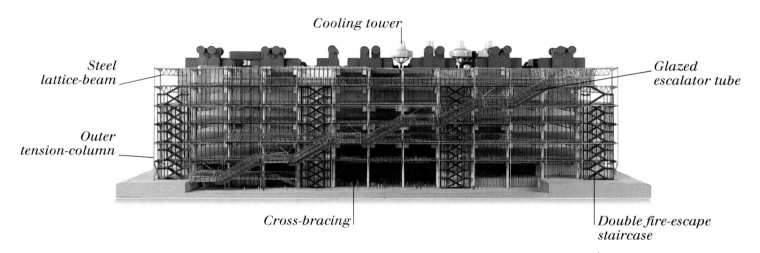

Cooling tower

Steel
lattice-beam

Glazed
escalator tube

Outer
tension-column

Cross-bracing

Double fire-escape
staircase

PRINCIPAL FACADE, CENTRE GEORGES POMPIDOU, PARIS, FRANCE, 1977

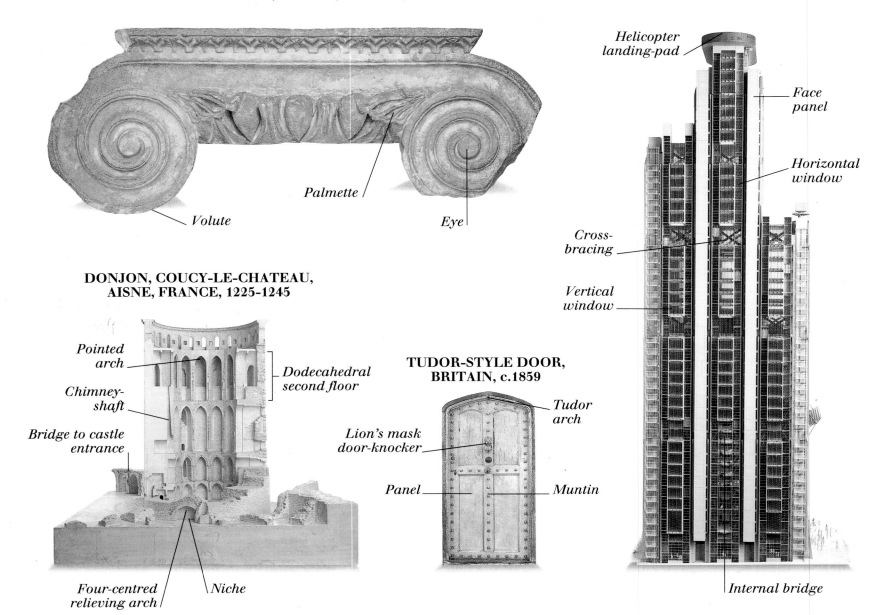

IONIC CAPITAL, THE PROPYLAEUM (GATEWAY), TEMPLE OF ATHENA POLIAS, PRIENE, GREECE, c.334 BC

Palmette

Volute

Eye

HONG KONG AND SHANGHAI BANK, HONG KONG, 1981-1985

Helicopter landing-pad

Face panel

Horizontal window

Cross-bracing

Vertical window

Internal bridge

DONJON, COUCY-LE-CHATEAU, AISNE, FRANCE, 1225-1245

Pointed arch

Chimney-shaft

Bridge to castle entrance

Dodecahedral second floor

Four-centred relieving arch

Niche

TUDOR-STYLE DOOR, BRITAIN, c.1859

Tudor arch

Lion's mask door-knocker

Panel

Muntin

CRYSTAL PALACE EXHIBITION HALL, LONDON, BRITAIN, 1851

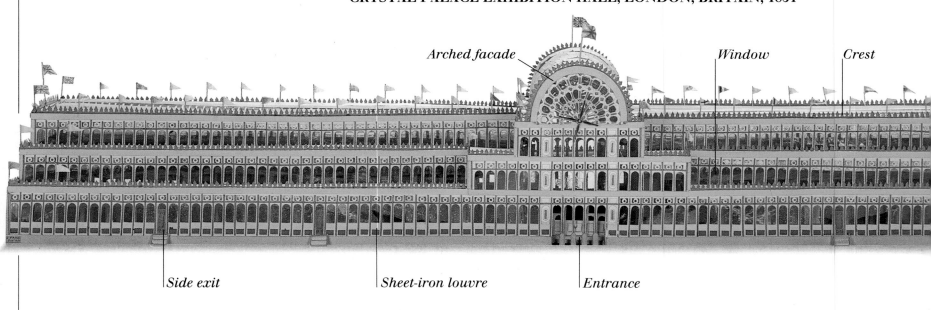

Arched facade

Window

Crest

Side exit

Sheet-iron louvre

Entrance

EYEWITNESS VISUAL DICTIONARIES

THE VISUAL
DICTIONARY *of*
BUILDINGS

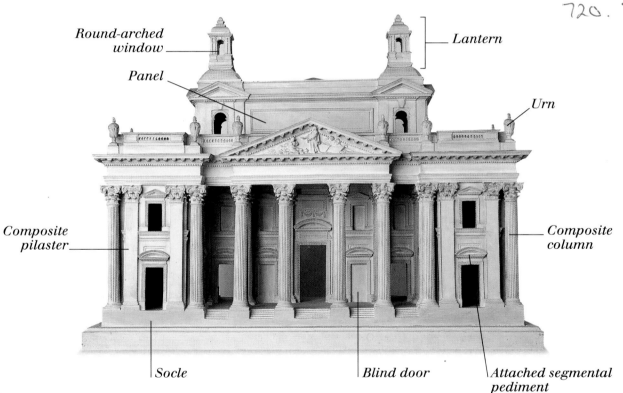

Round-arched window

Panel

Lantern

Urn

Composite pilaster

Composite column

Socle

Blind door

Attached segmental pediment

PROPOSED FACADE, THE MADELEINE, PARIS, FRANCE, 1764

DORLING KINDERSLEY
LONDON • NEW YORK • STUTTGART

A DORLING KINDERSLEY BOOK

PROJECT ART EDITOR NICOLA LIDDIARD
DESIGNER PAUL CALVER

PROJECT EDITOR ROGER TRITTON
EDITOR FIONA COURTENAY-THOMPSON
CONSULTANT EDITOR ALEXANDRA KENNEDY

MANAGING ART EDITOR STEPHEN KNOWLDEN
SENIOR EDITOR MARTYN PAGE
MANAGING EDITOR RUTH MIDGLEY

PHOTOGRAPHY TIM RIDLEY, ANDY CRAWFORD
ILLUSTRATIONS JOHN WOODCOCK, SIMONE END, KATHLEEN McDOUGALL

PRODUCTION HILARY STEPHENS

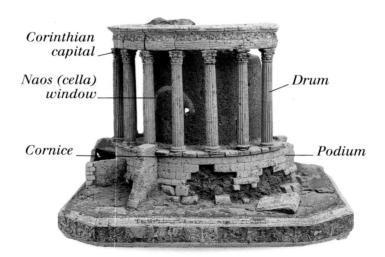

Corinthian capital

Naos (cella) window

Drum

Cornice

Podium

TEMPLE OF VESTA, TIVOLI, ITALY, c.80 BC

FIRST PUBLISHED IN GREAT BRITAIN IN 1992
BY DORLING KINDERSLEY LIMITED,
9 HENRIETTA STREET, LONDON WC2E 8PS

A CIP CATALOGUE RECORD FOR THIS BOOK IS AVAILABLE FROM THE BRITISH LIBRARY

ISBN 0-86318-961-X

REPRODUCED BY COLOURSCAN, SINGAPORE
PRINTED AND BOUND BY ARNOLDO MONDADORI, VERONA, ITALY

Contents

Palm leaf

Lotus stem

Lotus bud

PLANT CAPITAL OF THE PTOLEMAIC-ROMAN PERIOD, EGYPT, 332-30 BC

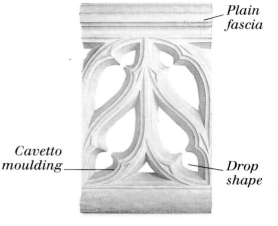

Plain fascia

Cavetto moulding

Drop shape

GOTHIC CURVILINEAR (FLOWING) TRACERY

ANCIENT EGYPT 6

ANCIENT GREECE 8

ANCIENT ROME 10

WALLS 14

ROOFS AND CHIMNEYS 16

MEDIEVAL CASTLES AND HOUSES 18

MEDIEVAL CHURCHES 20

GOTHIC 22

RENAISSANCE 26

BAROQUE AND NEOCLASSICAL 30

CEILINGS 36

ARCHES AND VAULTS 38

DOMES 40

ISLAMIC BUILDINGS 42

SOUTH AND EAST ASIA 44

DOORS 46

WINDOWS 48

THE 19TH CENTURY 50

THE EARLY 20TH CENTURY 52

MODERN BUILDINGS 54

ARCHITECTURAL STYLES 58

INDEX 60

ACKNOWLEDGMENTS 64

Circular moulding

VICTORIAN MOULDED BRICK

Arris

"RUBBER" (SOFT, EASILY-SPLIT) BRICK

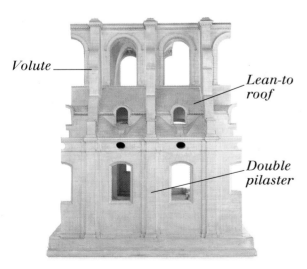

Round arch

Architrave

Socle

Barley-sugar column

ROUND ARCH AND BARLEY-SUGAR COLUMNS

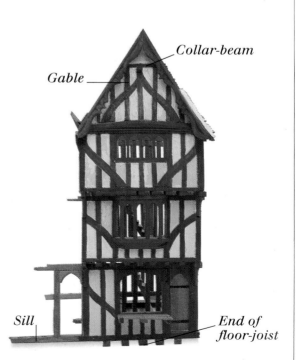

Collar-beam

Gable

Sill

End of floor-joist

TIMBER-FRAMED HOUSE, BRITAIN, c.1450

Volute

Lean-to roof

Double pilaster

CHURCH OF ST. PAUL-ST. LOUIS, PARIS, FRANCE, FROM 1627

Ancient Egypt

THE CIVILIZATION OF THE ANCIENT EGYPTIANS (which lasted from about 3100 BC until it was finally absorbed into the Roman empire in 30 BC) is famous for its temples and tombs. Egyptian temples were often huge and geometric, like the Temple of Amon-Re (below and right). They were usually decorated with hieroglyphs (sacred characters used for picture-writing) and painted reliefs depicting gods, Pharaohs (kings), and queens. Tombs were particularly important to the Egyptians, who believed that the dead were resurrected in the after-life. The tombs were often decorated – as, for example, the surround of the false door opposite – in order to give comfort to the dead. The best-known ancient Egyptian tombs are the pyramids (see pp. 58-59), which were designed to symbolize the rays of the sun. Many of the architectural forms used by the ancient Egyptians were later adopted by other civilizations; for example, columns and capitals were later used by the ancient Greeks (see pp. 8-9) and ancient Romans (see pp. 10-11).

Cornice decorated with cavetto moulding

Campaniform (open papyrus) capital

Architrave

Papyrus-bud capital

Socle

Side aisle *Central nave* *Side aisle*

SIDE VIEW OF HYPOSTYLE HALL, TEMPLE OF AMON-RE, KARNAK, EGYPT, c.1290 BC

Horus, the sun-god *Architrave* *Stone slab forming flat roof of side aisle*

Kepresh crown with disc

Chons, the moon-god *Amon-Re, king of the gods* *Hathor, the sky-goddess* *Papyrus motif* *Cartouche (oval border) containing the titles of the Pharaoh (king)* *Socle* *Aisle running north-south*

LIMESTONE FALSE DOOR WITH HIEROGLYPHS, TOMB OF KING TJETJI, GIZA, EGYPT, c.2400 BC

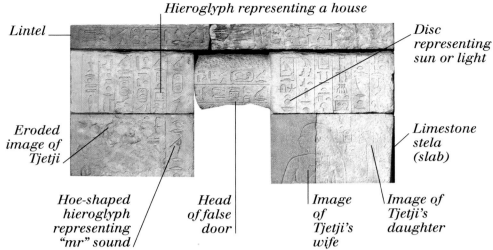

Lintel

Hieroglyph representing a house

Disc representing sun or light

Eroded image of Tjetji

Limestone stela (slab)

Hoe-shaped hieroglyph representing "mr" sound

Head of false door

Image of Tjetji's wife

Image of Tjetji's daughter

PLANT CAPITAL OF THE PTOLEMAIC-ROMAN PERIOD, EGYPT, 332-30 BC

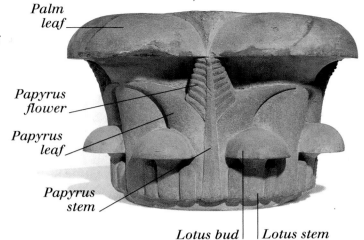

Palm leaf

Papyrus flower

Papyrus leaf

Papyrus stem

Lotus bud

Lotus stem

Cornice decorated with cavetto moulding

Bead moulding

Trellis window

Rectangular pier decorated with hieroglyphs

Elevated roof of central nave

Clerestory

Disc representing sun or light

Architrave

Square abacus

Papyrus-bud capital

Papyriform column

Shaft

Scene depicting a Pharaoh (king) paying homage to the god Amon-Re

Central nave

ANCIENT EGYPTIAN BUILDING DECORATION

DECORATED WINDOW, MEDINET HABU, EGYPT, c.1198 BC

ROPE AND PATERAE DECORATION

CAPITAL WITH THE HEAD OF THE SKY-GODDESS HATHOR, TEMPLE OF ISIS, PHILAE, EGYPT, 283-47 BC

LOTUS AND PAPYRUS FRIEZE DECORATION

Ancient Greece

THE CLASSICAL TEMPLES OF ANCIENT GREECE were built according to the belief that certain forms and proportions were pleasing to the gods. There were three main ancient Greek architectural orders (styles), which can be distinguished by the decoration and proportions of their columns, capitals (column tops), and entablatures (structures resting on the capitals). The oldest is the Doric order, which dates from the seventh century BC and was used mainly on the Greek mainland and in the western colonies, such as Sicily and southern Italy. The Temple of Neptune, shown here, is a classic example of this order. It is hypaethral (roofless) and peripteral (surrounded by a single row of columns). About a century later, the more decorative Ionic order developed on the Aegean Islands. Features of this order include volutes (spiral scrolls) on capitals and acroteria (pediment ornaments). The Corinthian order was invented in Athens in the fifth century BC and is typically identified by an acanthus leaf on the capitals. This order was later widely used in ancient Roman architecture.

CAPITALS OF THE THREE ORDERS OF ANCIENT GREEK ARCHITECTURE

Abacus

Echinus

Annulet

Trachelion (neck)

DORIC CAPITAL, THE PROPYLAEUM (GATEWAY), THE ACROPOLIS, ATHENS, GREECE, 449 BC

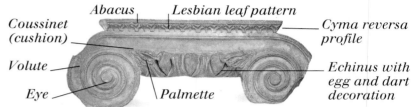

Abacus

Lesbian leaf pattern

Cyma reversa profile

Coussinet (cushion)

Volute

Echinus with egg and dart decoration

Eye

Palmette

IONIC CAPITAL, THE PROPYLAEUM (GATEWAY), TEMPLE OF ATHENA POLIAS, PRIENE, GREECE, c.334 BC

Mask

Abacus

Volute

Cauliculus

Acanthus leaf

Bell-shaped core

CORINTHIAN CAPITAL FROM A STOA (PORTICO), PROBABLY FROM ASIA MINOR

TEMPLE OF NEPTUNE, PAESTUM, ITALY, c.460 BC

Raking cornice

Trachelion (neck)   Taenia   Triglyph   Metope   Glyph (channel)

Pediment

Doric entablature

Pteron (external colonnade)

Euthynteria   Drum   Stylobate   Column of the Doric order

PLAN OF THE TEMPLE OF NEPTUNE, PAESTUM

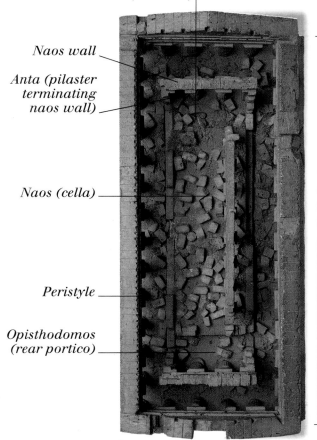

Pronaos (vestibule)

Naos wall

Anta (pilaster terminating naos wall)

Naos (cella)

Peristyle

Opisthodomos (rear portico)

Pteron (external colonnade)

Hexastyle pteron (colonnade of six columns)

ANCIENT GREEK BUILDING DECORATION

Volute

FACADE, TREASURY OF ATREUS, MYCENAE, GREECE, 1350-1250 BC

Meander

FRETWORK, PARTHENON, ATHENS, GREECE, 447-436 BC

ACROTERION, TEMPLE OF APHAIA, AEGINA, GREECE, 490 BC

Griffon (gryphon)

Raking cornice

ANTEFIXA, TEMPLE OF APHAIA, AEGINA, GREECE, 490 BC

Palmette

Volute

Regula (short fillet beneath taenia)

Eaves

Cornice

Frieze

Architrave

Capital

Shaft

Crepidoma (stepped base)

Entasis (slight curve of a column)

Intercolumniation

Fluting

Ancient Rome 1

IN THE EARLY PERIOD OF THE ROMAN EMPIRE extensive use was made of ancient Greek architectural ideas, particularly those of the Corinthian order (see pp. 8-9). As a result, many early Roman buildings – such as the Temple of Vesta (opposite) – closely resemble ancient Greek buildings. A distinctive Roman style began to evolve in the first century AD. This style developed the interiors of buildings (the Greeks had concentrated on the exterior) by using arches, vaults, and domes inside the buildings, and by ornamenting internal walls. Many of these features can be seen in the Pantheon. Exterior columns were often used for decorative, rather than structural, purposes, as in the Colosseum and the Porta Nigra (see pp. 12-13). Smaller buildings had timber frames with wattle-and-daub walls, as in the mill (see pp. 12-13). Roman architecture remained influential for many centuries, with some of its principles being used in the 11th century in Romanesque buildings (see pp. 20-21) and also in the 15th and 16th centuries in Renaissance buildings (see pp. 26-29).

ANCIENT ROMAN BUILDING DECORATION

FESTOON, TEMPLE OF VESTA, TIVOLI, ITALY, c.80 BC

RICHLY DECORATED ROMAN OVUM

INTERIOR OF THE PANTHEON, ROME, ITALY, 118-c.128

Inner dome, following the curve of a depressed arch

Outer saucer dome

Entablature

Curved cornice

Lesene

Cornice

Triangular pediment

Concave niche

Marble veneer

Segmental pediment

Pedestal

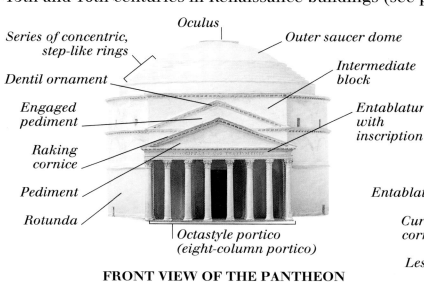

Series of concentric, step-like rings

Oculus

Outer saucer dome

Dentil ornament

Intermediate block

Engaged pediment

Entablature with inscription

Raking cornice

Pediment

Rotunda

Octastyle portico (eight-column portico)

FRONT VIEW OF THE PANTHEON

SIDE VIEW OF THE PANTHEON

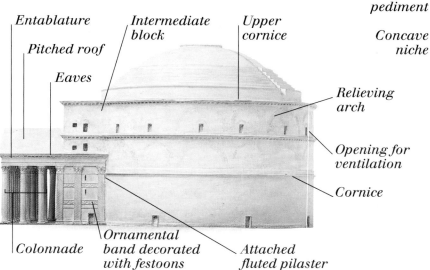

Entablature

Intermediate block

Upper cornice

Pitched roof

Eaves

Relieving arch

Opening for ventilation

Cornice

Colonnade

Ornamental band decorated with festoons

Attached fluted pilaster

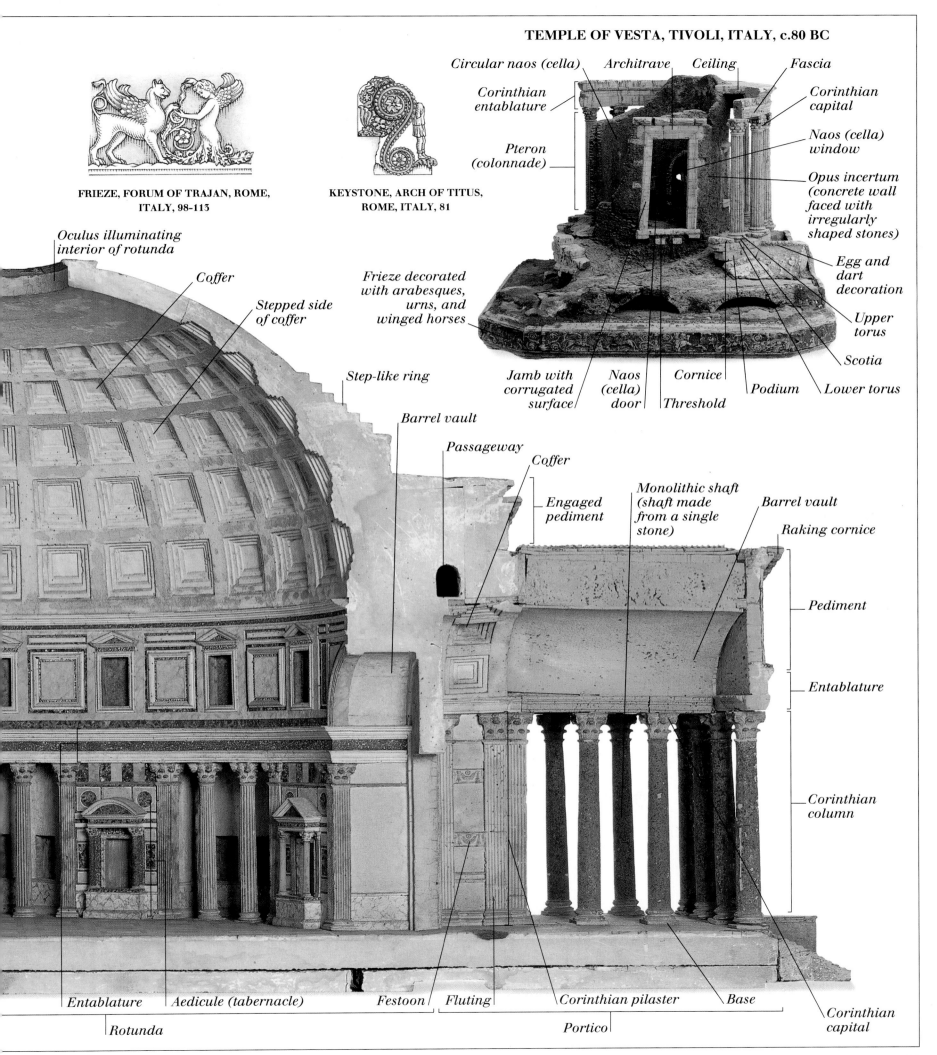

FRIEZE, FORUM OF TRAJAN, ROME,
ITALY, 98-113

KEYSTONE, ARCH OF TITUS,
ROME, ITALY, 81

TEMPLE OF VESTA, TIVOLI, ITALY, c.80 BC

Circular naos (cella)

Architrave

Ceiling

Fascia

Corinthian
entablature

Corinthian
capital

Naos (cella)
window

Pteron
(colonnade)

Opus incertum
(concrete wall
faced with
irregularly
shaped stones)

Oculus illuminating
interior of rotunda

Coffer

Stepped side
of coffer

Frieze decorated
with arabesques,
urns, and
winged horses

Egg and
dart
decoration

Upper
torus

Scotia

Step-like ring

Jamb with
corrugated
surface

Naos
(cella)
door

Cornice

Threshold

Podium

Lower torus

Barrel vault

Passageway

Coffer

Engaged
pediment

Monolithic shaft
(shaft made
from a single
stone)

Barrel vault

Raking cornice

Pediment

Entablature

Corinthian
column

Entablature

Aedicule (tabernacle)

Festoon

Fluting

Corinthian pilaster

Base

Corinthian
capital

Rotunda

Portico

11

Ancient Rome 2

SIDE VIEW OF A ROMAN MILL

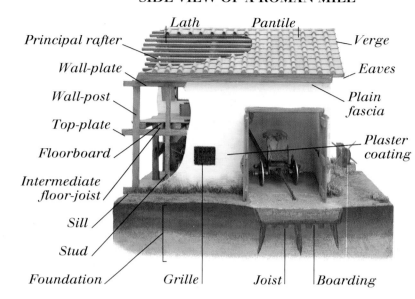

Lath
Pantile
Principal rafter
Verge
Wall-plate
Eaves
Wall-post
Plain fascia
Top-plate
Plaster coating
Floorboard
Intermediate floor-joist
Sill
Stud
Foundation
Grille
Joist
Boarding

FRONT VIEW OF A ROMAN MILL, 1ST CENTURY BC

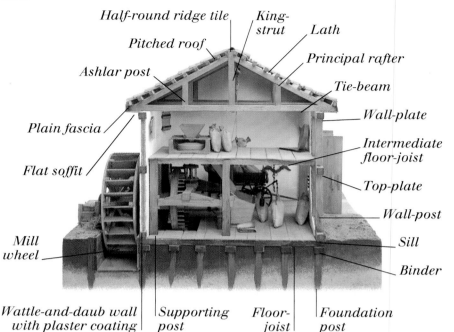

Half-round ridge tile
King-strut
Lath
Pitched roof
Principal rafter
Ashlar post
Tie-beam
Wall-plate
Plain fascia
Intermediate floor-joist
Flat soffit
Top-plate
Wall-post
Mill wheel
Sill
Binder
Wattle-and-daub wall with plaster coating
Supporting post
Floor-joist
Foundation post

THE COLOSSEUM (FLAVIAN AMPHITHEATRE), ROME, ITALY, 70-82

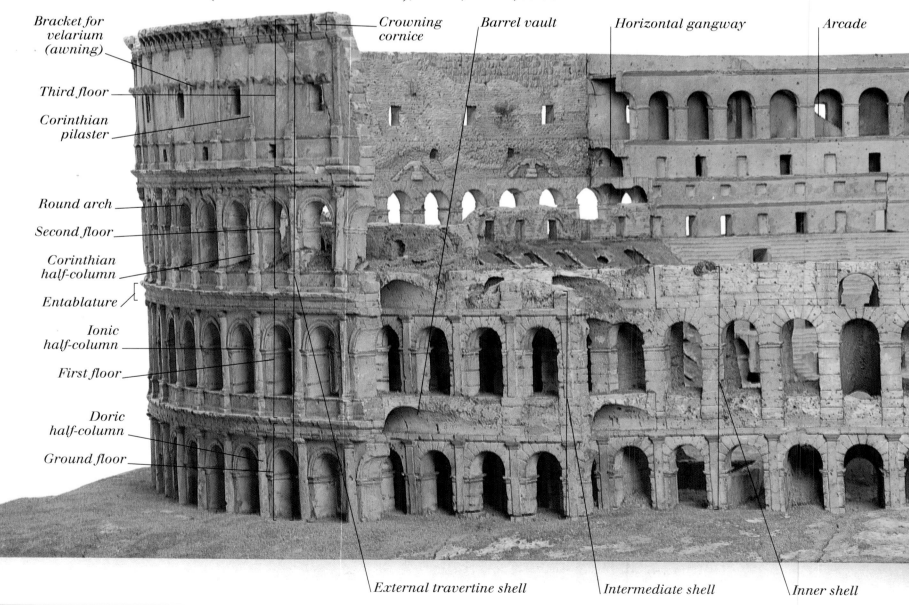

Bracket for velarium (awning)
Crowning cornice
Barrel vault
Horizontal gangway
Arcade
Third floor
Corinthian pilaster
Round arch
Second floor
Corinthian half-column
Entablature
Ionic half-column
First floor
Doric half-column
Ground floor
External travertine shell
Intermediate shell
Inner shell

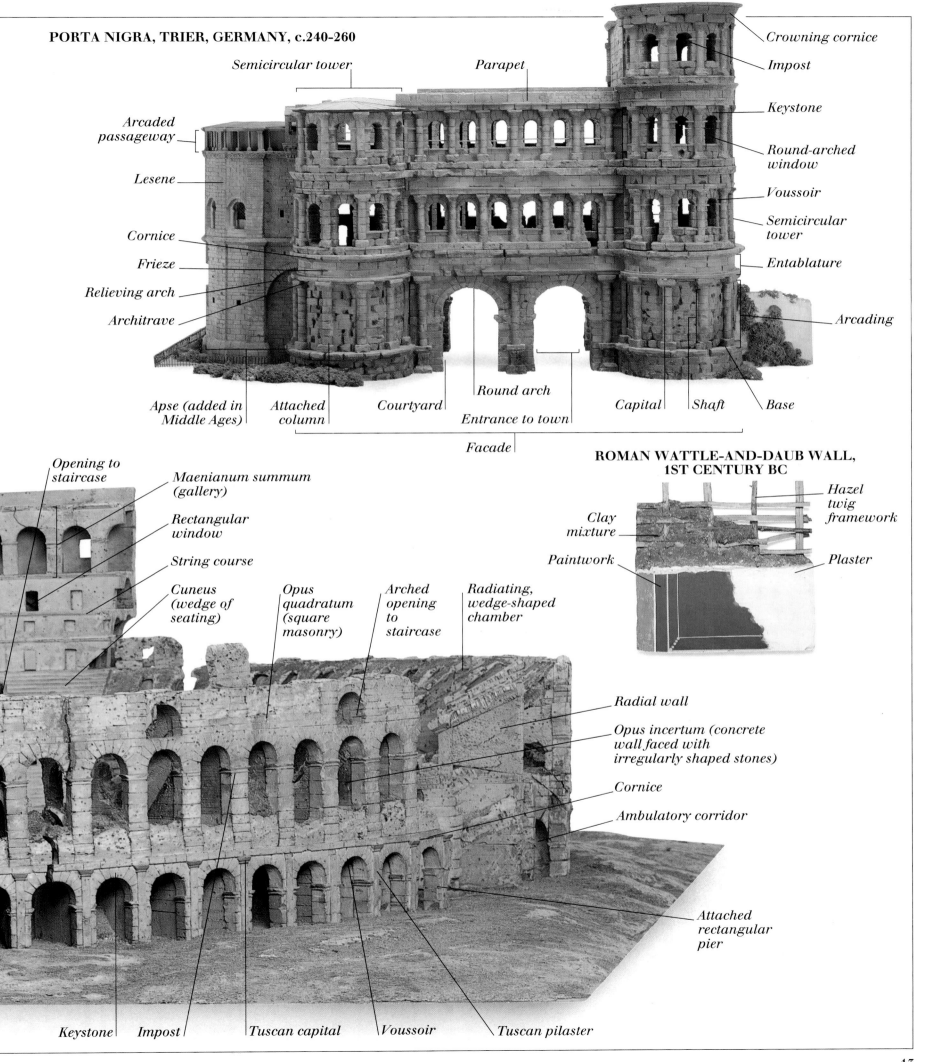

PORTA NIGRA, TRIER, GERMANY, c.240-260

Crowning cornice

Impost

Semicircular tower

Parapet

Keystone

Arcaded passageway

Round-arched window

Lesene

Voussoir

Semicircular tower

Cornice

Entablature

Frieze

Relieving arch

Architrave

Arcading

Apse (added in Middle Ages)

Attached column

Courtyard

Round arch

Capital

Shaft

Base

Entrance to town

Facade

ROMAN WATTLE-AND-DAUB WALL, 1ST CENTURY BC

Opening to staircase

Maenianum summum (gallery)

Hazel twig framework

Clay mixture

Rectangular window

String course

Paintwork

Plaster

Cuneus (wedge of seating)

Opus quadratum (square masonry)

Arched opening to staircase

Radiating, wedge-shaped chamber

Radial wall

Opus incertum (concrete wall faced with irregularly shaped stones)

Cornice

Ambulatory corridor

Attached rectangular pier

Keystone

Impost

Tuscan capital

Voussoir

Tuscan pilaster

Walls

A WALL IS A CONTINUOUS structure that encloses or subdivides a building. The two main types of load-bearing outer wall are frame-construction walls and mass-construction walls. Frame-construction walls have a frame of timber or metal. In timber-framed houses, such as the medieval house below, the open panels between the studs (vertical wall timbers) were filled with wattle (thin wooden laths) and daub (mud or clay). The finished house was often embellished with decorative braces and wooden carvings. A mass-construction wall is a solid structure made of brick or stone. Various types of bonding have been developed to increase the strength of brick walls. In English bond, bricks are laid so that alternate courses (layers) on the face of the wall are composed exclusively of either headers (bricks laid widthways) or stretchers (bricks laid lengthways). In Flemish bond, the face of each course consists of alternate headers and stretchers. Stretcher bond is composed of stretchers only. The walls of large buildings were usually built from stone. For example, in St. Paul's Cathedral (opposite), piers (solid masonry supports) bear the weight of huge arches and windows. These piers are decorated with columns and pilasters.

MEDIEVAL WOODEN WALL ORNAMENT, BRITAIN

WATTLE AND DAUB

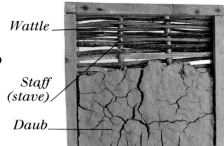

Wattle

Staff (stave)

Daub

BRICKLAYING FORMATIONS

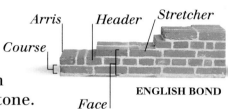

Arris

Header

Stretcher

Course

Face

ENGLISH BOND

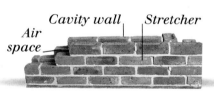

Bed-joint

Perpend

Closer

Header

Stretcher

FLEMISH BOND

Cavity wall

Stretcher

Air space

STRETCHER BOND

TYPES OF BRICK

SANDSTONE BRICK

FLINT FACING-BRICK

MASS-PRODUCED BRICK, BRITAIN, 19TH CENTURY

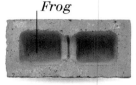

Frog

EARLY METRIC BRICK, BRITAIN, 19TH CENTURY

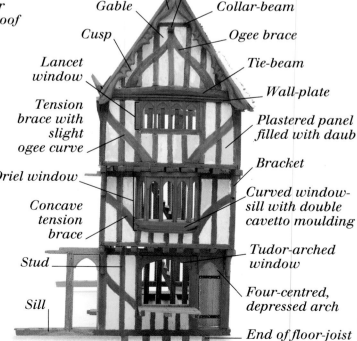

MODERN ENGINEERING BRICK

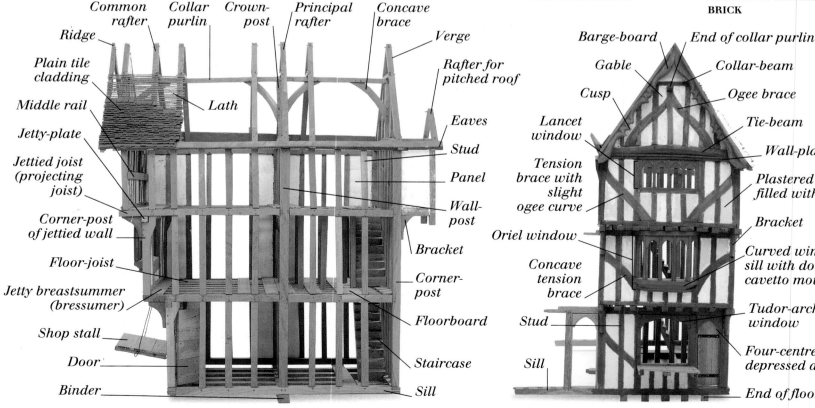

Common rafter

Collar purlin

Crown-post

Principal rafter

Concave brace

Ridge

Plain tile cladding

Middle rail

Jetty-plate

Jettied joist (projecting joist)

Corner-post of jettied wall

Floor-joist

Jetty breastsummer (bressumer)

Shop stall

Door

Binder

Lath

Verge

Rafter for pitched roof

Eaves

Stud

Panel

Wall-post

Bracket

Corner-post

Floorboard

Staircase

Sill

SIDE VIEW OF A TIMBER-FRAMED HOUSE, BRITAIN, c.1450

Barge-board

End of collar purlin

Gable

Collar-beam

Cusp

Ogee brace

Lancet window

Tie-beam

Tension brace with slight ogee curve

Wall-plate

Plastered panel filled with daub

Oriel window

Bracket

Concave tension brace

Curved window-sill with double cavetto moulding

Stud

Tudor-arched window

Sill

Four-centred, depressed arch

End of floor-joist

FRONT VIEW OF A TIMBER-FRAMED HOUSE

WOODEN RECONSTRUCTION OF A PIER, ST. PAUL'S CATHEDRAL, LONDON, BRITAIN, 1675-1710 (BY C. WREN)

Buttress

Air duct

Pedestal of outer dome

Corridor from inner dome to clerestory

Inner dome

Apex of relieving arch

Relieving arch

"Whispering Gallery"

Moulded bracket

Cornice

Saucer dome

Main vault

Pendentive

Arch cutting into main vault

Springing point of vault

Attached abutment pier

Cornice

Entablature

Coffered arch

Plain frieze

Cornice

Fascia

Composite capital

Panelling

Panelling

Main vessel

Floor level

Foundation (part of crypt)

Clerestory window

Exterior transept wall

Round arch

Semi-dome

Side-aisle vault

Round, transverse, side-aisle arch

Frieze with carvings of festoons

Composite pilaster

Side aisle

Base

Socle

VIEW FROM THE NAVE

Inner dome

Buttress

Passageway

Pedestal of outer dome

Cornice

Triangular buttress

Passageway along upper clerestory wall

Mullioned window

Segmental arch

Clerestory window

Exterior wall of main elevation

Side-aisle vault

Round arch over passageway

Round-arched hollow

Lunette

Festoon

Wreath carving

Inner dome

Semi-dome

Barrel vault

Cornice

Semi-dome

Barrel vault

Corinthian capital

Coffered arch

Entablature

Composite capital

Frieze

Composite pilaster

Panelling

Base

Socle

Floor level

Concave, round-arched niche

VIEW FROM A SIDE AISLE

15

Roofs and chimneys

A ROOF HAS TWO BASIC COMPONENTS: a covering and a supporting frame. In pitched (sloping) roofs, the frame consists of inclined rafters and horizontal purlins (timbers) connected to a roof truss by joints such as the mortise-and-tenon joint, or the edge-halfed scarf-joint. The most common roof coverings are slates, clay tiles, and asphalt (used to waterproof flat roofs), although thatch and lead are still used, mainly to roof old buildings. A thatched roof consists of layered bundles of straw or reeds, which are attached to the roof with steel or hazel rods, and fixed in place by crooks (hooks) driven into the rafters. A chimney consists of a passage (or flue) for the escape of fumes from a fireplace; a chimney-stack, which projects above the roof; and a chimney-pot on top of the stack. Chimney-pots and chimney-stacks sometimes have elaborate designs, some of which are shown opposite.

ROOF FINIAL

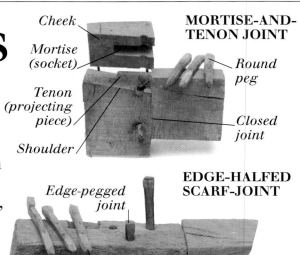

MORTISE-AND-TENON JOINT

Cheek
Mortise (socket)
Tenon (projecting piece)
Shoulder
Round peg
Closed joint

EDGE-HALFED SCARF-JOINT

Edge-pegged joint
Square peg

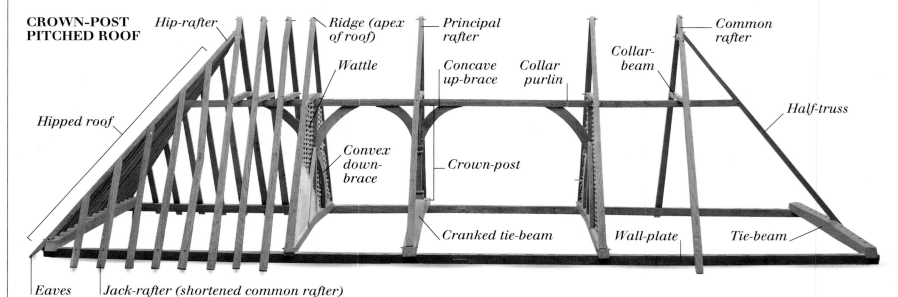

CROWN-POST PITCHED ROOF

Hip-rafter
Ridge (apex of roof)
Principal rafter
Common rafter
Wattle
Concave up-brace
Collar purlin
Collar-beam
Hipped roof
Half-truss
Convex down-brace
Crown-post
Cranked tie-beam
Wall-plate
Tie-beam
Eaves
Jack-rafter (shortened common rafter)

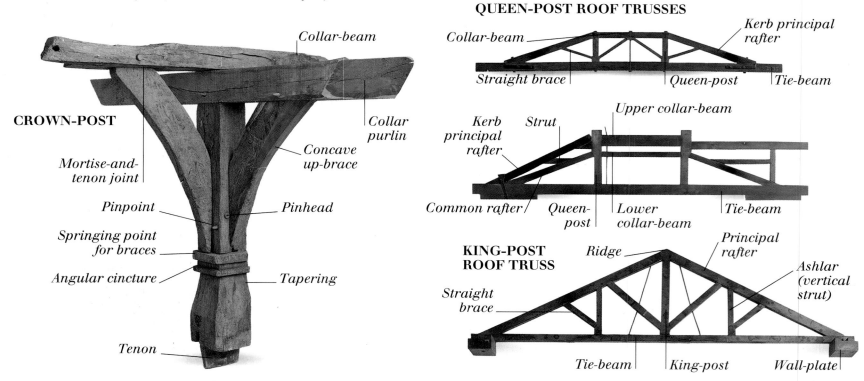

CROWN-POST

Collar-beam
Collar purlin
Concave up-brace
Mortise-and-tenon joint
Pinpoint
Pinhead
Springing point for braces
Angular cincture
Tapering
Tenon

QUEEN-POST ROOF TRUSSES

Collar-beam
Kerb principal rafter
Straight brace
Queen-post
Tie-beam

Kerb principal rafter
Strut
Upper collar-beam
Common rafter
Queen-post
Lower collar-beam
Tie-beam

KING-POST ROOF TRUSS

Ridge
Principal rafter
Ashlar (vertical strut)
Straight brace
Tie-beam
King-post
Wall-plate

TYPES OF ROOF

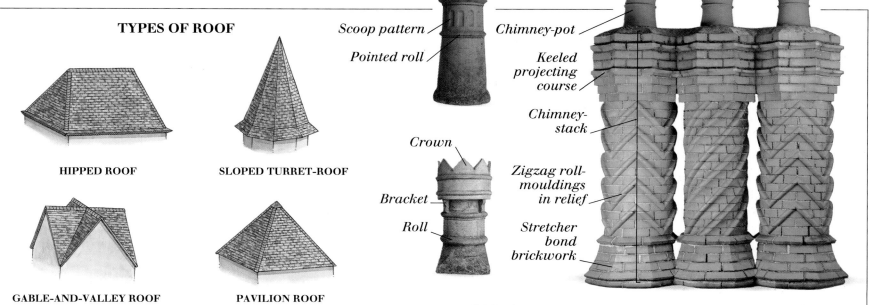

HIPPED ROOF

SLOPED TURRET-ROOF

GABLE-AND-VALLEY ROOF

PAVILION ROOF

Scoop pattern

Pointed roll

Chimney-pot

Keeled projecting course

Crown

Chimney-stack

Bracket

Roll

Zigzag roll-mouldings in relief

Stretcher bond brickwork

VICTORIAN CHIMNEY-POTS AND CHIMNEY-STACKS

THATCHED ROOF

TILED ROOF

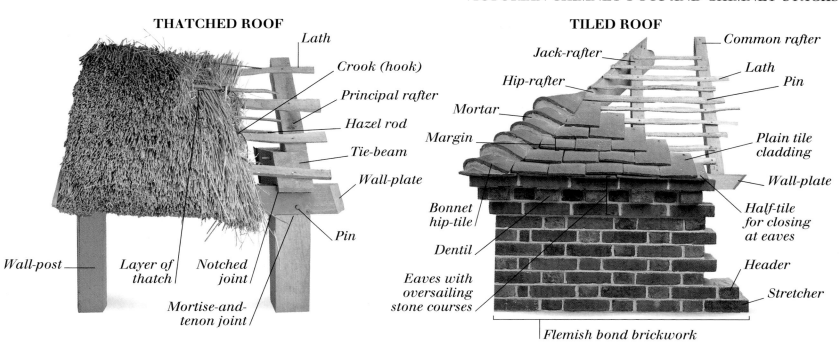

Lath

Crook (hook)

Principal rafter

Hazel rod

Tie-beam

Wall-plate

Pin

Wall-post

Layer of thatch

Notched joint

Mortise-and-tenon joint

Jack-rafter

Hip-rafter

Mortar

Margin

Bonnet hip-tile

Dentil

Eaves with oversailing stone courses

Common rafter

Lath

Pin

Plain tile cladding

Wall-plate

Half-tile for closing at eaves

Header

Stretcher

Flemish bond brickwork

TYPES OF ROOF TILE

JOINTS FOR LEAD ROOFS

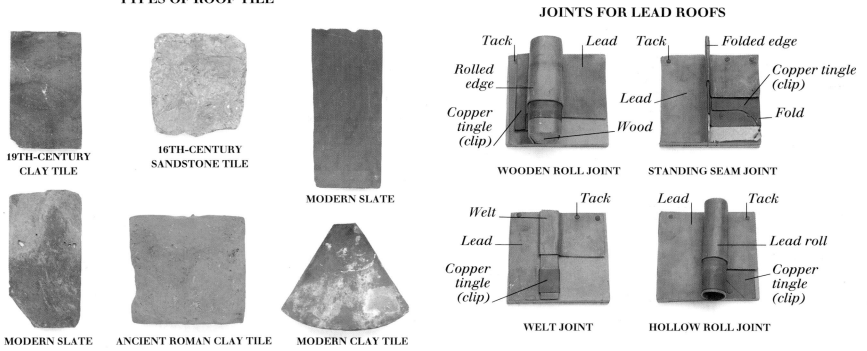

19TH-CENTURY CLAY TILE

16TH-CENTURY SANDSTONE TILE

MODERN SLATE

MODERN SLATE

ANCIENT ROMAN CLAY TILE

MODERN CLAY TILE

Tack

Lead

Rolled edge

Copper tingle (clip)

Tack

Folded edge

Copper tingle (clip)

Lead

Fold

Wood

WOODEN ROLL JOINT

STANDING SEAM JOINT

Welt

Lead

Copper tingle (clip)

Tack

Lead

Tack

Lead roll

Copper tingle (clip)

WELT JOINT

HOLLOW ROLL JOINT

Medieval castles and houses

WARFARE WAS COMMON IN EUROPE in the Middle Ages, and many monarchs and nobles built castles as a form of defence. Typical medieval castles have outer walls surrounding a moat. Inside the moat is a bailey (courtyard), protected by a chemise (jacket-wall). The innermost and strongest part of a medieval castle is the keep. There are two main types of keep: towers called donjons, such as the Tour de César and Coucy-le-Château, and rectangular keeps ("hall-keeps"), such as the Tower of London. Castles were often guarded by salients (projecting fortifications), like those of the Bastille. Medieval houses typically had timber cruck (tent-like) frames, wattle-and-daub walls (see pp. 14-15), and pitched roofs, like those on medieval London Bridge (opposite).

DONJON, TOUR DE CESAR, PROVINS, FRANCE, 12TH CENTURY

- Loophole
- Oculus
- Battlements (crenellations)
- Conical spire
- Hemispherical cupola
- Flying buttress
- Gallery
- Hexahedral hall
- Squinch
- Semicircular turret
- Vaulted room
- Fireplace
- Main entrance
- Bailey
- Staircase to chemise (jacket-wall)
- Embrasure
- Chemise (jacket-wall)
- Plain impost
- Depressed cupola
- Vaulted staircase
- Motte

- Blind, rounded relieving arch
- Merlon
- Battlements (crenellations)
- Tetrahedral spire
- Crenel
- Loophole
- Rectangular turret
- Wooden staircase leading to entrance above ground level
- Quoin
- Timber-framed house
- Cornice
- Buttress
- Round-arched window with twin openings
- Cruck frame
- Paling

TOWER OF LONDON, BRITAIN, FROM 1070

- Loophole

SALIENT, CAERNARVON CASTLE, BRITAIN, 1283-1323

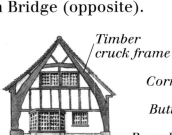

- Timber cruck frame

CRUCK-FRAMED HOUSE, BRITAIN, c.1200

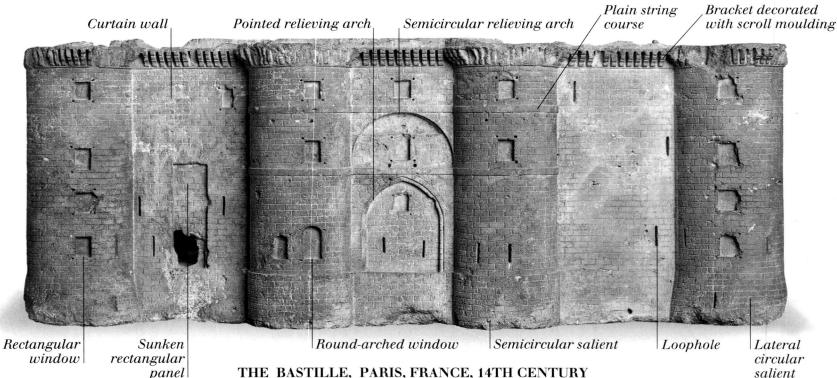

- Curtain wall
- Pointed relieving arch
- Semicircular relieving arch
- Plain string course
- Bracket decorated with scroll moulding
- Rectangular window
- Sunken rectangular panel
- Round-arched window
- Semicircular salient
- Loophole
- Lateral circular salient

THE BASTILLE, PARIS, FRANCE, 14TH CENTURY

MEDIEVAL LONDON BRIDGE, BRITAIN, 1176 (WITH 14TH-CENTURY BATTLEMENTED BUILDING, NONESUCH HOUSE, AND TWO-TOWERED GATE)

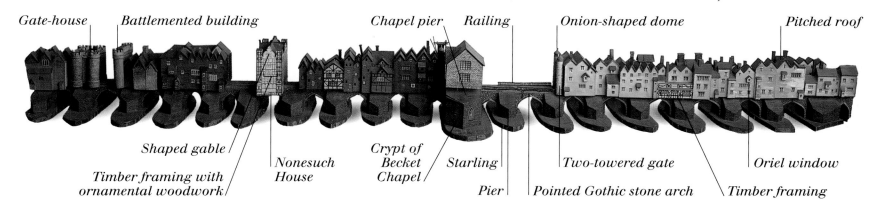

Gate-house

Battlemented building

Chapel pier

Railing

Onion-shaped dome

Pitched roof

Shaped gable

Nonesuch House

Timber framing with ornamental woodwork

Crypt of Becket Chapel

Starling

Pier

Two-towered gate

Pointed Gothic stone arch

Oriel window

Timber framing

DONJON, COUCY-LE-CHATEAU, AISNE, FRANCE, 1225-1245

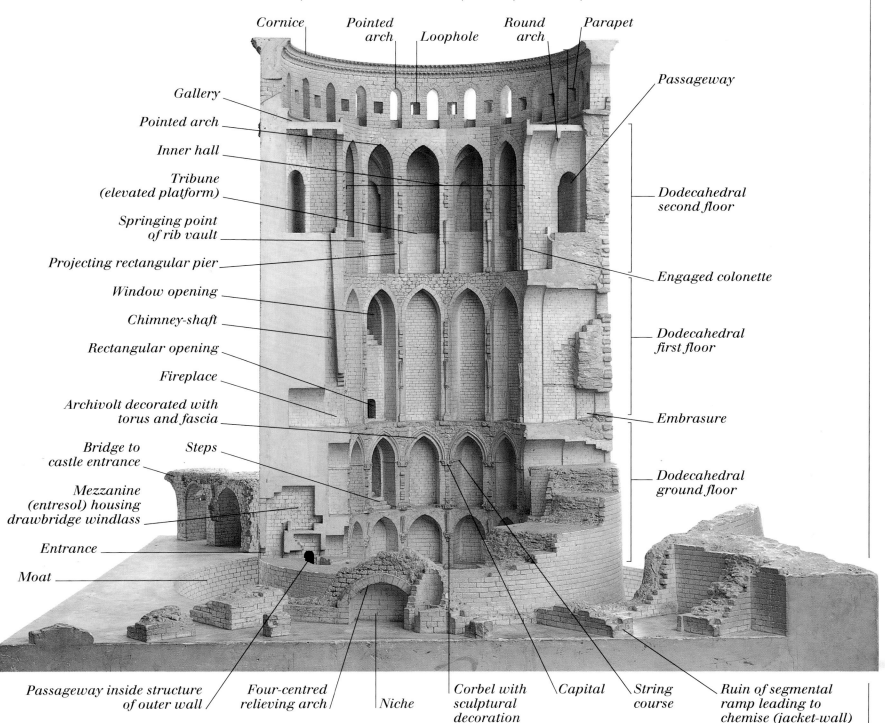

Cornice

Pointed arch

Loophole

Round arch

Parapet

Gallery

Passageway

Pointed arch

Inner hall

Tribune (elevated platform)

Dodecahedral second floor

Springing point of rib vault

Projecting rectangular pier

Engaged colonette

Window opening

Chimney-shaft

Dodecahedral first floor

Rectangular opening

Fireplace

Archivolt decorated with torus and fascia

Embrasure

Bridge to castle entrance

Steps

Dodecahedral ground floor

Mezzanine (entresol) housing drawbridge windlass

Entrance

Moat

Passageway inside structure of outer wall

Four-centred relieving arch

Niche

Corbel with sculptural decoration

Capital

String course

Ruin of segmental ramp leading to chemise (jacket-wall)

Medieval churches

DURING THE MIDDLE AGES, large numbers of churches were built in Europe. European churches of this period typically have high vaults supported by massive piers and columns. In the 10th century, the Romanesque style developed. Romanesque architects adopted many Roman or early Christian architectural ideas, such as cross-shaped ground-plans – like that of Angoulême Cathedral (opposite) – and the basilican system of a nave with a central vessel and side aisles. In the mid-12th century, flying buttresses and pointed vaults appeared. These features later became widely used in Gothic architecture (see pp. 22-23). Bagneux Church (opposite) has both styles: a Romanesque tower, and a Gothic nave and choir.

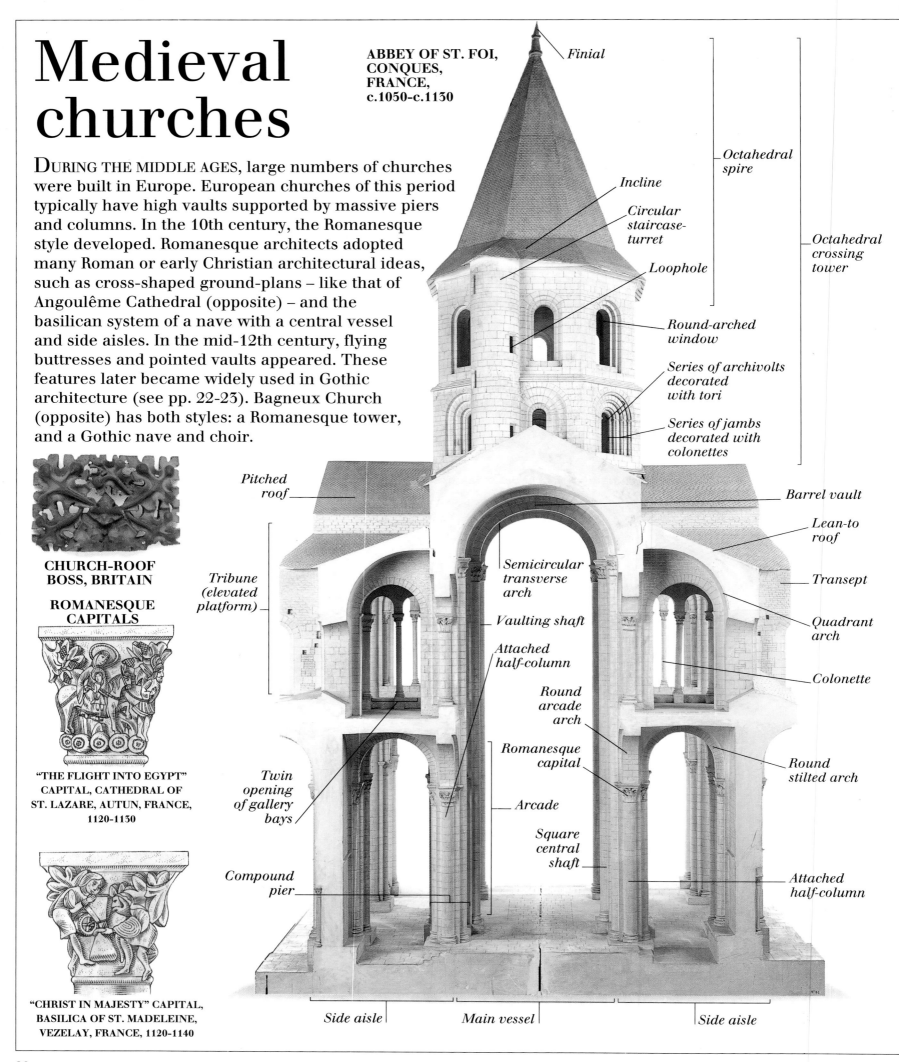

CHURCH-ROOF BOSS, BRITAIN

ROMANESQUE CAPITALS

"THE FLIGHT INTO EGYPT" CAPITAL, CATHEDRAL OF ST. LAZARE, AUTUN, FRANCE, 1120-1130

"CHRIST IN MAJESTY" CAPITAL, BASILICA OF ST. MADELEINE, VEZELAY, FRANCE, 1120-1140

ABBEY OF ST. FOI, CONQUES, FRANCE, c.1050-c.1130

Finial

Octahedral spire

Incline

Circular staircase-turret

Loophole

Octahedral crossing tower

Round-arched window

Series of archivolts decorated with tori

Series of jambs decorated with colonettes

Pitched roof

Barrel vault

Lean-to roof

Tribune (elevated platform)

Semicircular transverse arch

Transept

Vaulting shaft

Quadrant arch

Attached half-column

Colonette

Round arcade arch

Twin opening of gallery bays

Romanesque capital

Round stilted arch

Arcade

Compound pier

Square central shaft

Attached half-column

Side aisle

Main vessel

Side aisle

GROUND-PLAN OF ANGOULEME CATHEDRAL, FRANCE, FROM c.1105

Heavily moulded transverse arch

Crossing

Transept chapel

Chevet (choir with round apse and chapels)

Transept

Engaged column

Dome

Buttress

Nave

Transverse arch with plain fascia

Nave bay

Clustered column

Vestibule

CHOIR, CHURCH OF ST. SERGE, ANGERS, FRANCE, c.1215-1220

Historiated boss

Longitudinal ridge-rib

Loophole

Cell

Gable

Diagonal rib with torus moulding

Transverse arch

Domed rib-vault

Historiated keystone

Lierne

Formeret

Tas-de-charge

Round-arched window

Polyhedral abacus

Cubic abacus

Foliated capital

Attached colonette

Embrasure

Rectangular apse

Cornice

Vaulting shaft

Rectangular side-chapel

Impost with foliated frieze

Arcade column

Bay of main vessel

Octahedral socle

BAGNEUX CHURCH, FRANCE, 1170-1190

Moulded rib with an arris between two tori

Flying buttress

Roof space

Cell

Polyhedral abacus

Transverse arch

Oculus

Tower vault

Square-roofed pinnacle

Lean-to roof

Exterior wall

Triforium

Tower

Foliated capital

Pointed arch

Triple vaulting-shaft

Torus moulding

Quadripartite vault

Colonette

Formeret

Tower-vault oculus

Attached compound pier

Recessed panel

Corbel

Round arch

Pier buttress

Impost

Embrasure

Pier supporting tower

Weathering

Side aisle

Attached half-column

Base

Square socle

Intrados of arch with flat band between two tori

Nave column

Compound pier

Arcade

Nave

Choir

Octahedral socle

Bay

Attached colonette

21

Gothic 1

GOTHIC STAINED GLASS ON WOODEN FORM, WITH FOLIATED SCROLL MOTIF

GOTHIC BUILDINGS are characterized by rib vaults, pointed or lancet arches, flying buttresses, decorative tracery and gables, and stained-glass windows. Typical Gothic buildings include the Cathedrals of Salisbury and old St. Paul's in England, and Notre Dame de Paris in France (see pp. 24-25). The Gothic style developed out of Romanesque architecture in France (see pp. 20-21) in the mid-12th century, and then spread throughout Europe. The decorative elements of Gothic architecture became highly developed in buildings of the English Decorated style (late 13th-14th century) and the French Flamboyant style (15th-16th century). These styles are exemplified by the tower of Salisbury Cathedral and the staircase in the Church of St. Maclou (see pp. 24-25) respectively. In both of these styles, embellishments such as ballflowers and curvilinear (flowing) tracery were used liberally. The English Perpendicular style (late 14th-15th century), which followed the Decorated style, emphasized the vertical and horizontal elements of a building. A notable feature of this style is the hammer-beam roof.

GROUND-PLAN OF SALISBURY CATHEDRAL

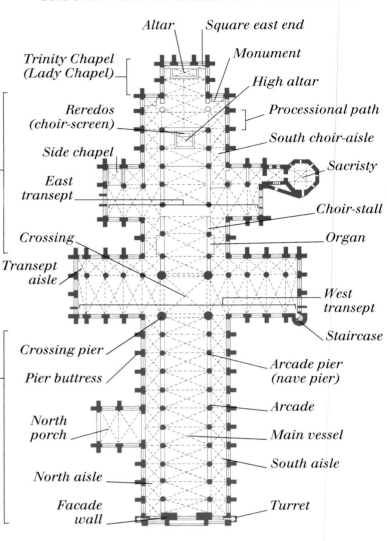

Altar
Square east end
Trinity Chapel (Lady Chapel)
Monument
High altar
Reredos (choir-screen)
Processional path
Side chapel
South choir-aisle
Choir
East transept
Sacristy
Choir-stall
Crossing
Organ
Transept aisle
West transept
Crossing pier
Staircase
Pier buttress
Arcade pier (nave pier)
Nave
Arcade
North porch
Main vessel
North aisle
South aisle
Facade wall
Turret

GOTHIC TORUS WITH BALLFLOWERS

Limestone block
Block members carved into rolls
Block members cut polygonally

Pencil guideline

Early stage of ballflower carving

BLOCK AFTER INITIAL CUTTING

BLOCK WITH MEMBERS CUT INTO ROLLS

Torus
Ballflower
Fillet
Mason's mark

FINISHED BLOCK

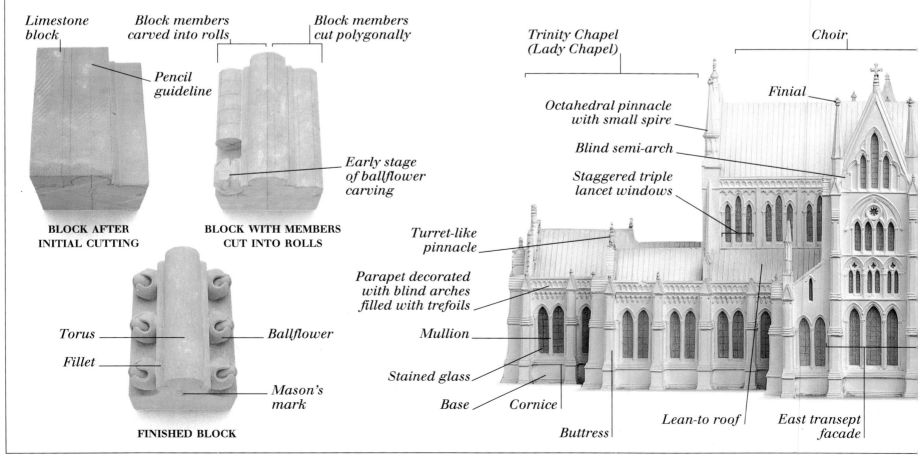

Trinity Chapel (Lady Chapel)
Choir

Octahedral pinnacle with small spire
Finial

Blind semi-arch

Staggered triple lancet windows

Turret-like pinnacle

Parapet decorated with blind arches filled with trefoils

Mullion

Stained glass

Base
Cornice
Buttress
Lean-to roof
East transept facade

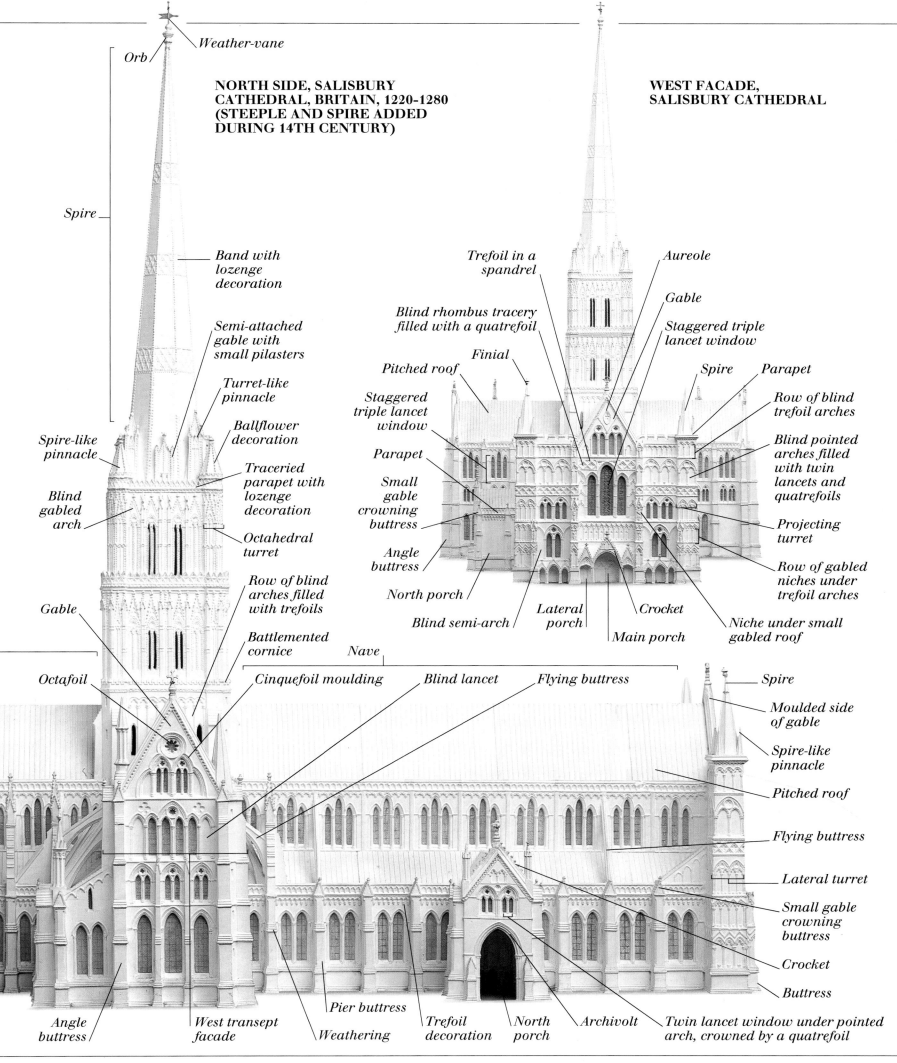

NORTH SIDE, SALISBURY CATHEDRAL, BRITAIN, 1220-1280 (STEEPLE AND SPIRE ADDED DURING 14TH CENTURY)

WEST FACADE, SALISBURY CATHEDRAL

Orb

Weather-vane

Spire

Band with lozenge decoration

Semi-attached gable with small pilasters

Turret-like pinnacle

Ballflower decoration

Spire-like pinnacle

Traceried parapet with lozenge decoration

Blind gabled arch

Octahedral turret

Row of blind arches filled with trefoils

Gable

Battlemented cornice

Octafoil

Cinquefoil moulding

Nave

Blind lancet

Flying buttress

Trefoil in a spandrel

Blind rhombus tracery filled with a quatrefoil

Finial

Pitched roof

Staggered triple lancet window

Parapet

Small gable crowning buttress

Angle buttress

North porch

Blind semi-arch

Lateral porch

Main porch

Crocket

Aureole

Gable

Staggered triple lancet window

Spire

Parapet

Row of blind trefoil arches

Blind pointed arches filled with twin lancets and quatrefoils

Projecting turret

Row of gabled niches under trefoil arches

Niche under small gabled roof

Spire

Moulded side of gable

Spire-like pinnacle

Pitched roof

Flying buttress

Lateral turret

Small gable crowning buttress

Crocket

Buttress

Angle buttress

West transept facade

Weathering

Pier buttress

Trefoil decoration

North porch

Archivolt

Twin lancet window under pointed arch, crowned by a quatrefoil

Gothic 2

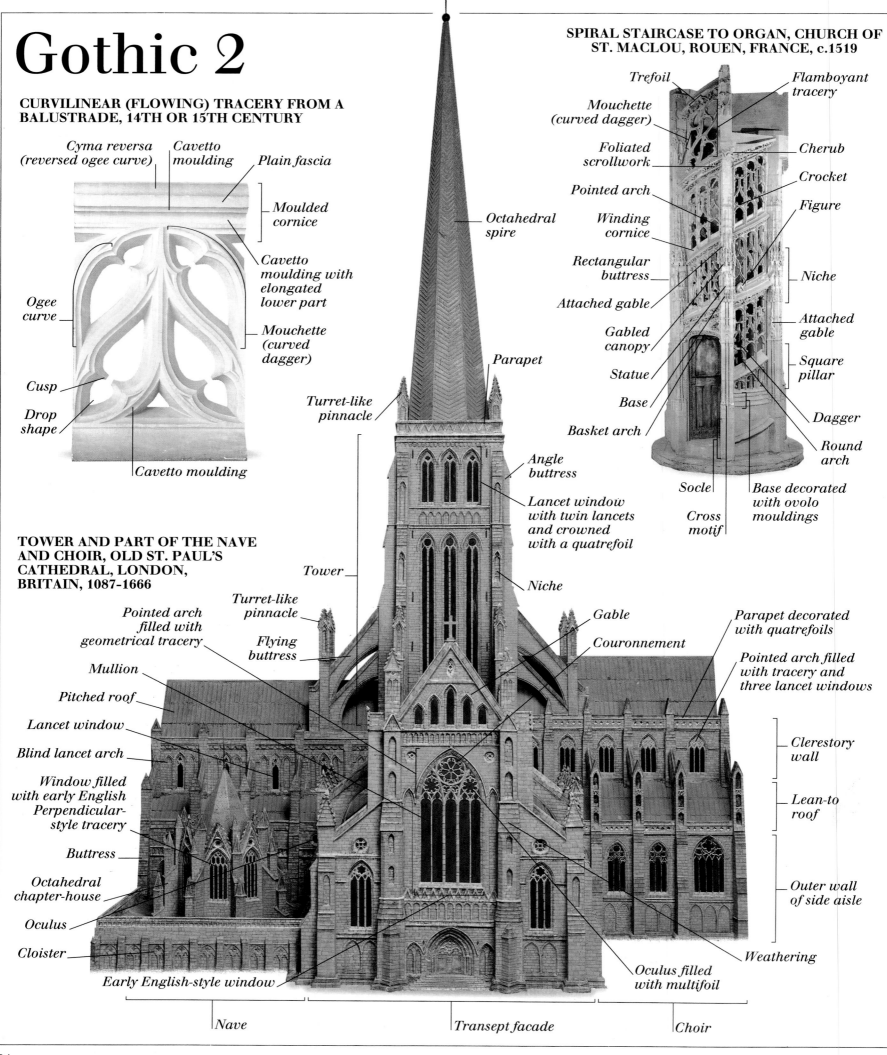

CURVILINEAR (FLOWING) TRACERY FROM A BALUSTRADE, 14TH OR 15TH CENTURY

Cyma reversa (reversed ogee curve)

Cavetto moulding

Plain fascia

Moulded cornice

Cavetto moulding with elongated lower part

Mouchette (curved dagger)

Ogee curve

Cusp

Drop shape

Cavetto moulding

SPIRAL STAIRCASE TO ORGAN, CHURCH OF ST. MACLOU, ROUEN, FRANCE, c.1519

Trefoil

Flamboyant tracery

Mouchette (curved dagger)

Cherub

Foliated scrollwork

Crocket

Pointed arch

Figure

Winding cornice

Rectangular buttress

Niche

Attached gable

Attached gable

Gabled canopy

Square pillar

Statue

Base

Dagger

Basket arch

Round arch

Socle

Base decorated with ovolo mouldings

Cross motif

Octahedral spire

Parapet

Turret-like pinnacle

Angle buttress

Lancet window with twin lancets and crowned with a quatrefoil

Niche

TOWER AND PART OF THE NAVE AND CHOIR, OLD ST. PAUL'S CATHEDRAL, LONDON, BRITAIN, 1087-1666

Tower

Pointed arch filled with geometrical tracery

Turret-like pinnacle

Flying buttress

Mullion

Gable

Couronnement

Parapet decorated with quatrefoils

Pointed arch filled with tracery and three lancet windows

Pitched roof

Lancet window

Blind lancet arch

Clerestory wall

Window filled with early English Perpendicular-style tracery

Lean-to roof

Buttress

Octahedral chapter-house

Outer wall of side aisle

Oculus

Cloister

Weathering

Early English-style window

Oculus filled with multifoil

Nave

Transept facade

Choir

24

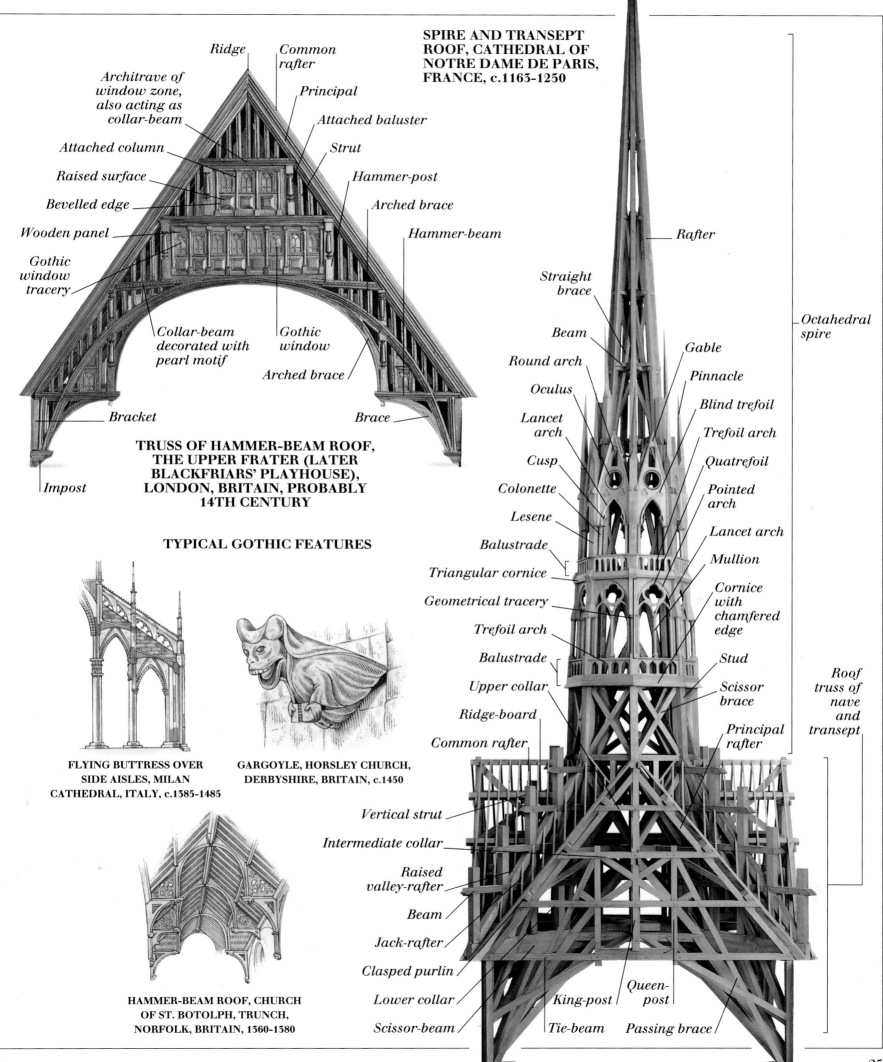

Ridge

Common rafter

Architrave of window zone, also acting as collar-beam

Principal

Attached baluster

Attached column

Strut

Raised surface

Hammer-post

Bevelled edge

Arched brace

Wooden panel

Hammer-beam

Gothic window tracery

Collar-beam decorated with pearl motif

Gothic window

Arched brace

Bracket

Brace

Impost

TRUSS OF HAMMER-BEAM ROOF, THE UPPER FRATER (LATER BLACKFRIARS' PLAYHOUSE), LONDON, BRITAIN, PROBABLY 14TH CENTURY

SPIRE AND TRANSEPT ROOF, CATHEDRAL OF NOTRE DAME DE PARIS, FRANCE, c.1163-1250

Rafter

Straight brace

Beam

Gable

Round arch

Pinnacle

Oculus

Blind trefoil

Lancet arch

Trefoil arch

Cusp

Quatrefoil

Colonette

Pointed arch

Lesene

Lancet arch

Balustrade

Mullion

Triangular cornice

Cornice with chamfered edge

Geometrical tracery

Trefoil arch

Balustrade

Stud

Upper collar

Scissor brace

Ridge-board

Principal rafter

Common rafter

Octahedral spire

Roof truss of nave and transept

Vertical strut

Intermediate collar

Raised valley-rafter

Beam

Jack-rafter

Clasped purlin

Lower collar

King-post

Queen-post

Scissor-beam

Tie-beam

Passing brace

TYPICAL GOTHIC FEATURES

FLYING BUTTRESS OVER SIDE AISLES, MILAN CATHEDRAL, ITALY, c.1385-1485

GARGOYLE, HORSLEY CHURCH, DERBYSHIRE, BRITAIN, c.1450

HAMMER-BEAM ROOF, CHURCH OF ST. BOTOLPH, TRUNCH, NORFOLK, BRITAIN, 1360-1380

Renaissance 1

THE RENAISSANCE was a European movement – lasting roughly from the 14th century to the mid-17th century – in which the arts and sciences underwent great changes. In architecture, these changes were marked by a return to the classical forms and proportions of ancient Roman buildings. The Renaissance originated in Italy, and the buildings most characteristic of its style can be found there, such as the Palazzo Strozzi shown here. Mannerism is a branch of the Renaissance style that distorts the classical forms; an example is the Laurentian Library staircase. As the Renaissance style spread to other European countries, many of its features were incorporated into the local architecture; for example, the Château de Montal in France (see pp. 28-29) incorporates aedicules (tabernacles).

FACADE ON TO PIAZZA, PALAZZO STROZZI

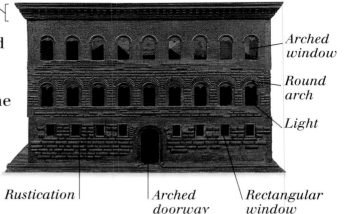

Crowning cornice

Arched window

Round arch

Light

Rustication

Arched doorway

Rectangular window

SIDE VIEW OF PALAZZO STROZZI, FLORENCE, ITALY, 1489 (BY G. DA SANGALLO, B. DA MAIANO, AND CRONACA)

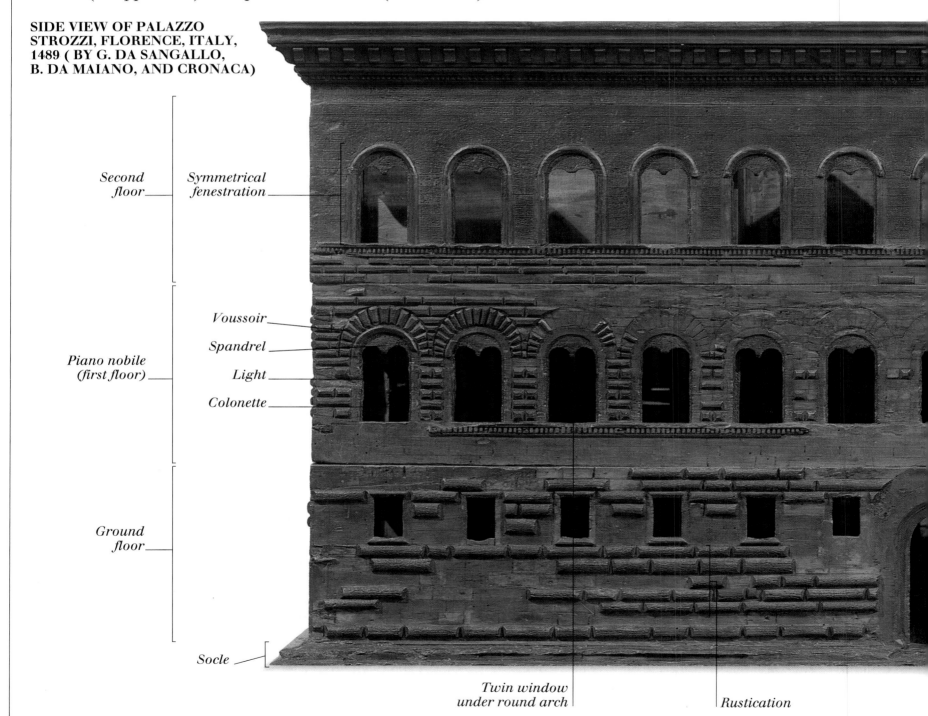

Second floor

Symmetrical fenestration

Voussoir

Spandrel

Light

Colonette

Piano nobile (first floor)

Ground floor

Socle

Twin window under round arch

Rustication

DETAILS FROM ITALIAN RENAISSANCE BUILDINGS

**PANEL FROM DRUM OF DOME,
FLORENCE CATHEDRAL, 1420-1436**

**COFFERING IN DOME,
PAZZI CHAPEL,
FLORENCE, 1429-1461**

**STAIRCASE,
LAURENTIAN LIBRARY,
FLORENCE, 1559**

**PORTICO, VILLA ROTUNDA,
VICENZA, 1567-1569**

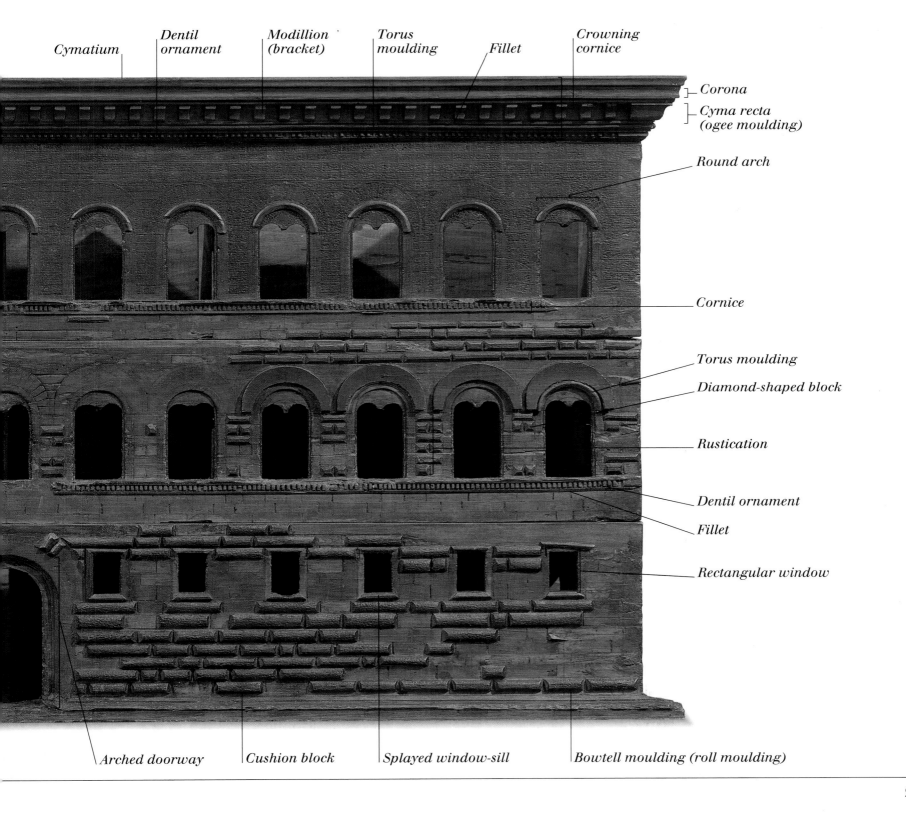

Cymatium

Dentil ornament

Modillion (bracket)

Torus moulding

Fillet

Crowning cornice

Corona

Cyma recta (ogee moulding)

Round arch

Cornice

Torus moulding

Diamond-shaped block

Rustication

Dentil ornament

Fillet

Rectangular window

Arched doorway

Cushion block

Splayed window-sill

Bowtell moulding (roll moulding)

27

Renaissance 2

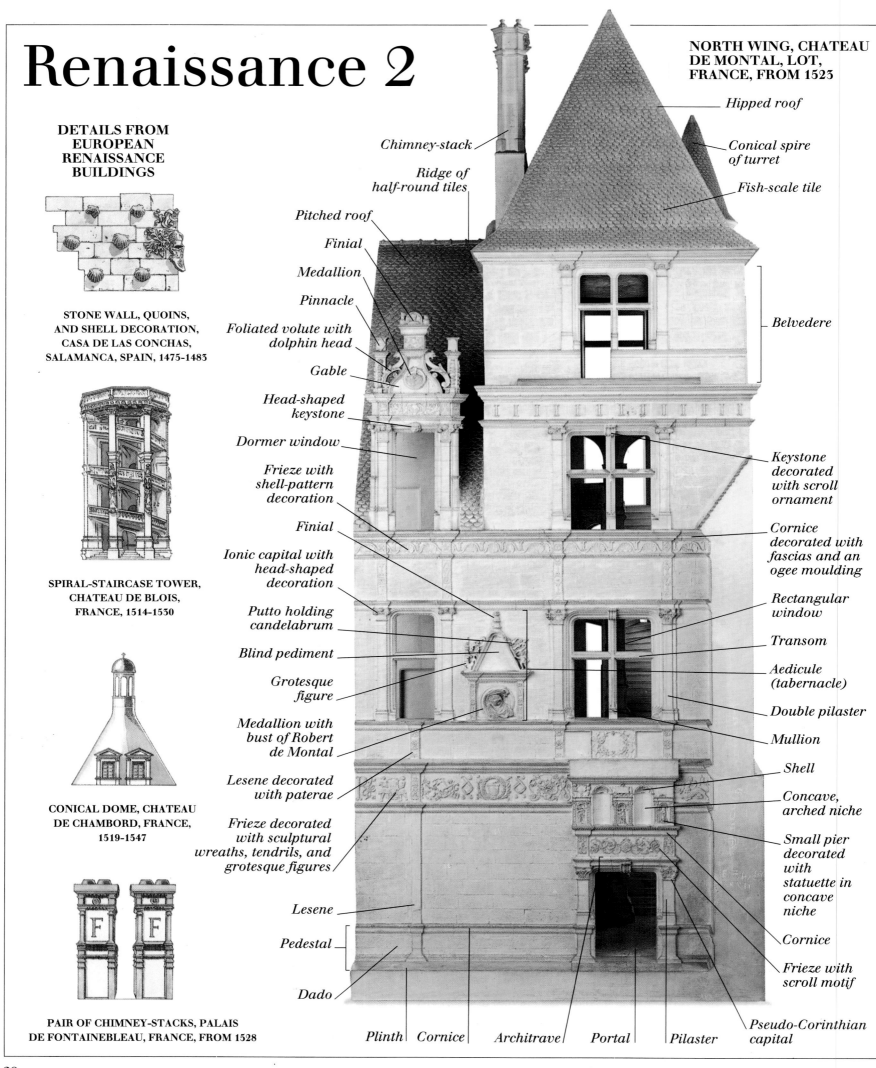

DETAILS FROM EUROPEAN RENAISSANCE BUILDINGS

STONE WALL, QUOINS, AND SHELL DECORATION, CASA DE LAS CONCHAS, SALAMANCA, SPAIN, 1475-1483

SPIRAL-STAIRCASE TOWER, CHATEAU DE BLOIS, FRANCE, 1514-1530

CONICAL DOME, CHATEAU DE CHAMBORD, FRANCE, 1519-1547

PAIR OF CHIMNEY-STACKS, PALAIS DE FONTAINEBLEAU, FRANCE, FROM 1528

Hipped roof

Conical spire of turret

Fish-scale tile

Chimney-stack

Ridge of half-round tiles

Pitched roof

Finial

Medallion

Pinnacle

Foliated volute with dolphin head

Gable

Head-shaped keystone

Dormer window

Frieze with shell-pattern decoration

Finial

Ionic capital with head-shaped decoration

Putto holding candelabrum

Blind pediment

Grotesque figure

Medallion with bust of Robert de Montal

Lesene decorated with paterae

Frieze decorated with sculptural wreaths, tendrils, and grotesque figures

Lesene

Pedestal

Dado

Belvedere

Keystone decorated with scroll ornament

Cornice decorated with fascias and an ogee moulding

Rectangular window

Transom

Aedicule (tabernacle)

Double pilaster

Mullion

Shell

Concave, arched niche

Small pier decorated with statuette in concave niche

Cornice

Frieze with scroll motif

Plinth Cornice Architrave Portal Pilaster Pseudo-Corinthian capital

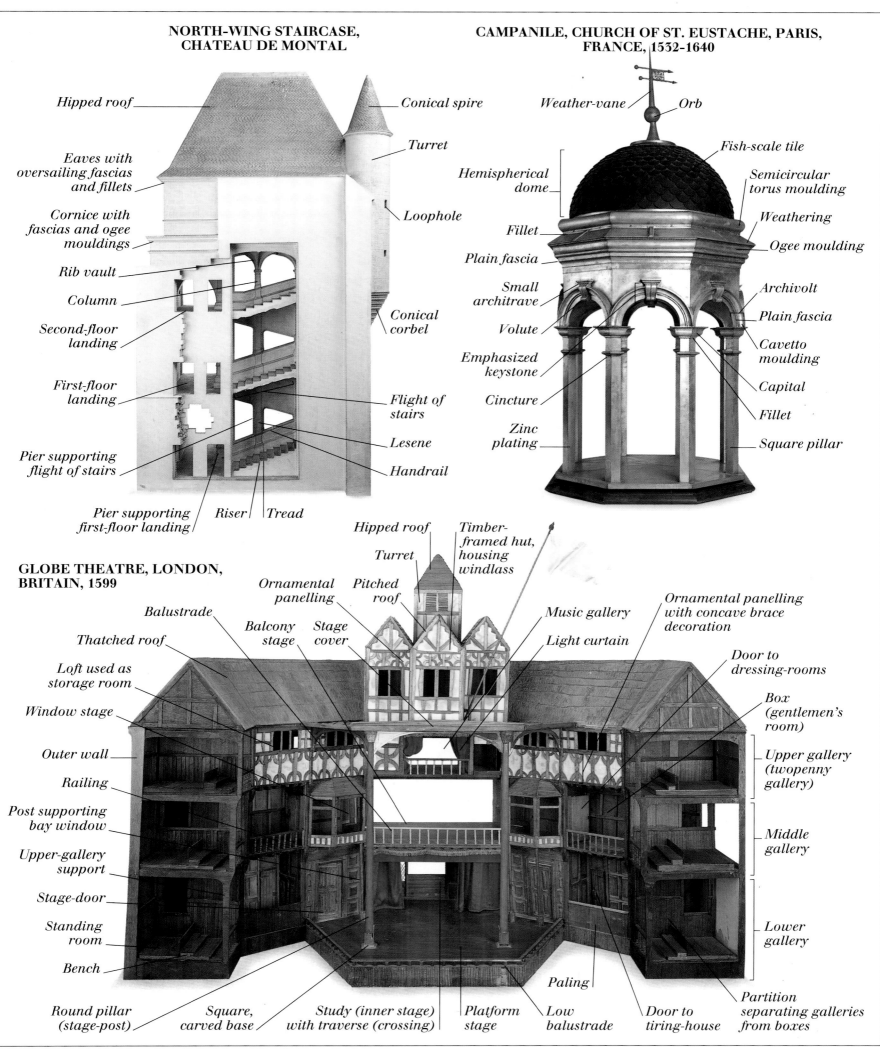

NORTH-WING STAIRCASE, CHATEAU DE MONTAL

Hipped roof

Eaves with oversailing fascias and fillets

Cornice with fascias and ogee mouldings

Rib vault

Column

Second-floor landing

First-floor landing

Pier supporting flight of stairs

Pier supporting first-floor landing

Riser

Tread

Conical spire

Turret

Loophole

Conical corbel

Flight of stairs

Lesene

Handrail

CAMPANILE, CHURCH OF ST. EUSTACHE, PARIS, FRANCE, 1532-1640

Weather-vane

Orb

Hemispherical dome

Fillet

Plain fascia

Small architrave

Volute

Emphasized keystone

Cincture

Zinc plating

Fish-scale tile

Semicircular torus moulding

Weathering

Ogee moulding

Archivolt

Plain fascia

Cavetto moulding

Capital

Fillet

Square pillar

GLOBE THEATRE, LONDON, BRITAIN, 1599

Balustrade

Thatched roof

Loft used as storage room

Window stage

Outer wall

Railing

Post supporting bay window

Upper-gallery support

Stage-door

Standing room

Bench

Round pillar (stage-post)

Square, carved base

Study (inner stage) with traverse (crossing)

Balcony stage

Stage cover

Ornamental panelling

Hipped roof

Turret

Pitched roof

Timber-framed hut, housing windlass

Music gallery

Light curtain

Ornamental panelling with concave brace decoration

Door to dressing-rooms

Box (gentlemen's room)

Upper gallery (twopenny gallery)

Middle gallery

Lower gallery

Partition separating galleries from boxes

Door to tiring-house

Paling

Low balustrade

Platform stage

Baroque and neoclassical 1

THE BAROQUE STYLE EVOLVED IN THE EARLY 17TH CENTURY in Rome. It is characterized by curved outlines and ostentatious decoration, as can be seen in the Italian church details (right). The baroque style was particularly widely favoured in Italy, Spain, and Germany. It was also adopted in Britain and France, but with adaptations. The British architects Sir Christopher Wren and Nicholas Hawksmoor, for example, used baroque features – such as the concave walls of St. Paul's Cathedral and the curved buttresses of the Church of St. George in the East (see pp. 32-33) – but they did so with restraint. Similarly, the curved buttresses and volutes of the Parisian Church of St. Paul-St. Louis are relatively plain. In the second half of the 17th century, a distinct classical style (known as neoclassicism) developed in northern Europe as a reaction to the excesses of baroque. Typical of this new style were churches such as the Madeleine (a proposed facade is shown below), as well as secular buildings such as the Cirque Napoleon (opposite) and the buildings of the British architect Sir John Soane (see pp. 34-35). In early 18th-century France, an extremely lavish form of baroque developed, known as rococo. The balcony from Nantes (see pp. 34-35) with its twisted ironwork and head-shaped corbels is typical of this style.

SCROLLED BUTTRESS, CHURCH OF ST. MARIA DELLA SALUTE, VENICE, 1631-1682

STATUE OF THE ECSTASY OF ST. THERESA, CHURCH OF ST. MARIA DELLA VITTORIA, ROME, 1645-1652

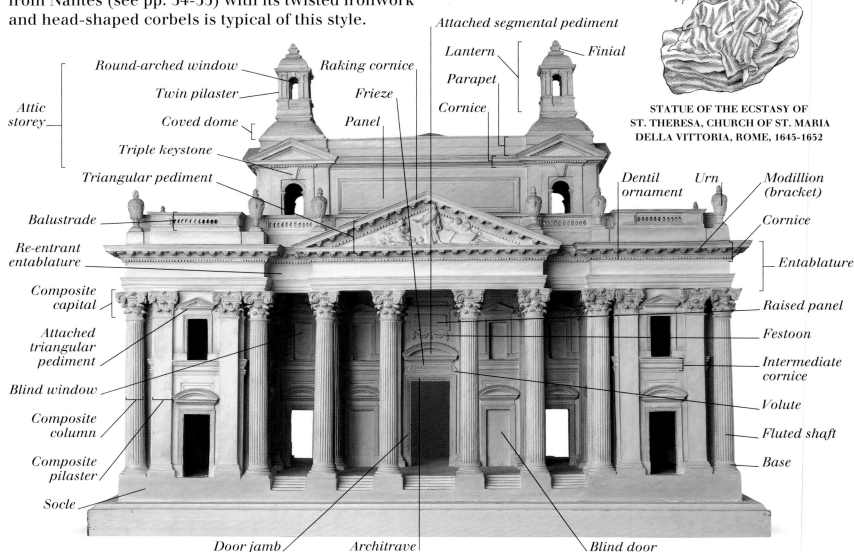

PROPOSED FACADE, THE MADELEINE (NEOCLASSICAL), PARIS, FRANCE, 1764 (BY P. CONTANT D'IVRY)

Labels on the facade illustration:

- Round-arched window
- Twin pilaster
- Attic storey
- Coved dome
- Triple keystone
- Triangular pediment
- Balustrade
- Re-entrant entablature
- Composite capital
- Attached triangular pediment
- Blind window
- Composite column
- Composite pilaster
- Socle
- Raking cornice
- Frieze
- Panel
- Attached segmental pediment
- Lantern
- Parapet
- Cornice
- Finial
- Dentil ornament
- Urn
- Modillion (bracket)
- Cornice
- Entablature
- Raised panel
- Festoon
- Intermediate cornice
- Volute
- Fluted shaft
- Base
- Door jamb
- Architrave
- Blind door

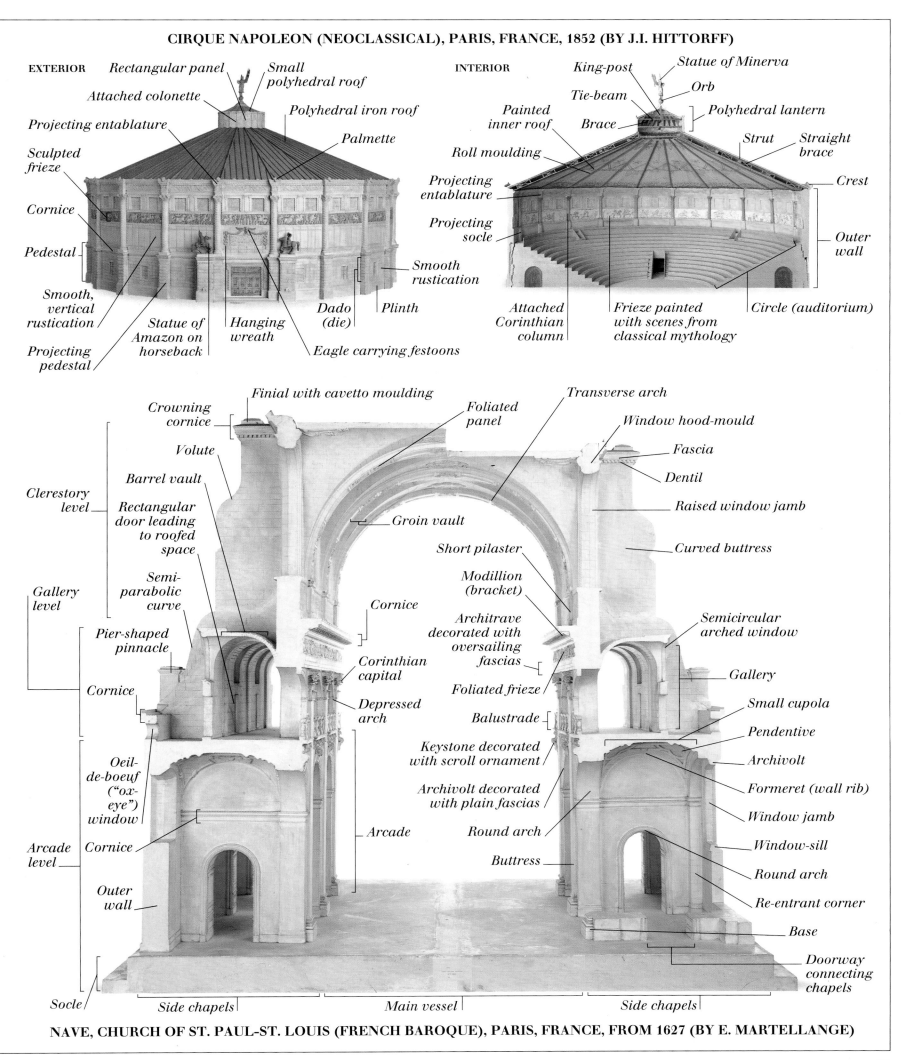

CIRQUE NAPOLEON (NEOCLASSICAL), PARIS, FRANCE, 1852 (BY J.I. HITTORFF)

EXTERIOR

Rectangular panel

Small polyhedral roof

Attached colonette

Polyhedral iron roof

Projecting entablature

Palmette

Sculpted frieze

Cornice

Pedestal

Smooth, vertical rustication

Statue of Amazon on horseback

Hanging wreath

Smooth rustication

Projecting pedestal

Dado (die)

Plinth

Eagle carrying festoons

INTERIOR

King-post

Statue of Minerva

Tie-beam

Orb

Brace

Polyhedral lantern

Painted inner roof

Strut

Straight brace

Roll moulding

Crest

Projecting entablature

Projecting socle

Outer wall

Attached Corinthian column

Frieze painted with scenes from classical mythology

Circle (auditorium)

Finial with cavetto moulding

Transverse arch

Crowning cornice

Foliated panel

Window hood-mould

Volute

Fascia

Barrel vault

Dentil

Clerestory level

Groin vault

Raised window jamb

Rectangular door leading to roofed space

Short pilaster

Curved buttress

Gallery level

Semi-parabolic curve

Modillion (bracket)

Cornice

Pier-shaped pinnacle

Architrave decorated with oversailing fascias

Semicircular arched window

Corinthian capital

Cornice

Foliated frieze

Gallery

Depressed arch

Small cupola

Oeil-de-boeuf ("ox-eye") window

Balustrade

Pendentive

Archivolt

Cornice

Keystone decorated with scroll ornament

Formeret (wall rib)

Arcade level

Arcade

Archivolt decorated with plain fascias

Window jamb

Outer wall

Round arch

Window-sill

Buttress

Round arch

Re-entrant corner

Base

Doorway connecting chapels

Socle

Side chapels

Main vessel

Side chapels

NAVE, CHURCH OF ST. PAUL-ST. LOUIS (FRENCH BAROQUE), PARIS, FRANCE, FROM 1627 (BY E. MARTELLANGE)

Baroque and neoclassical 2

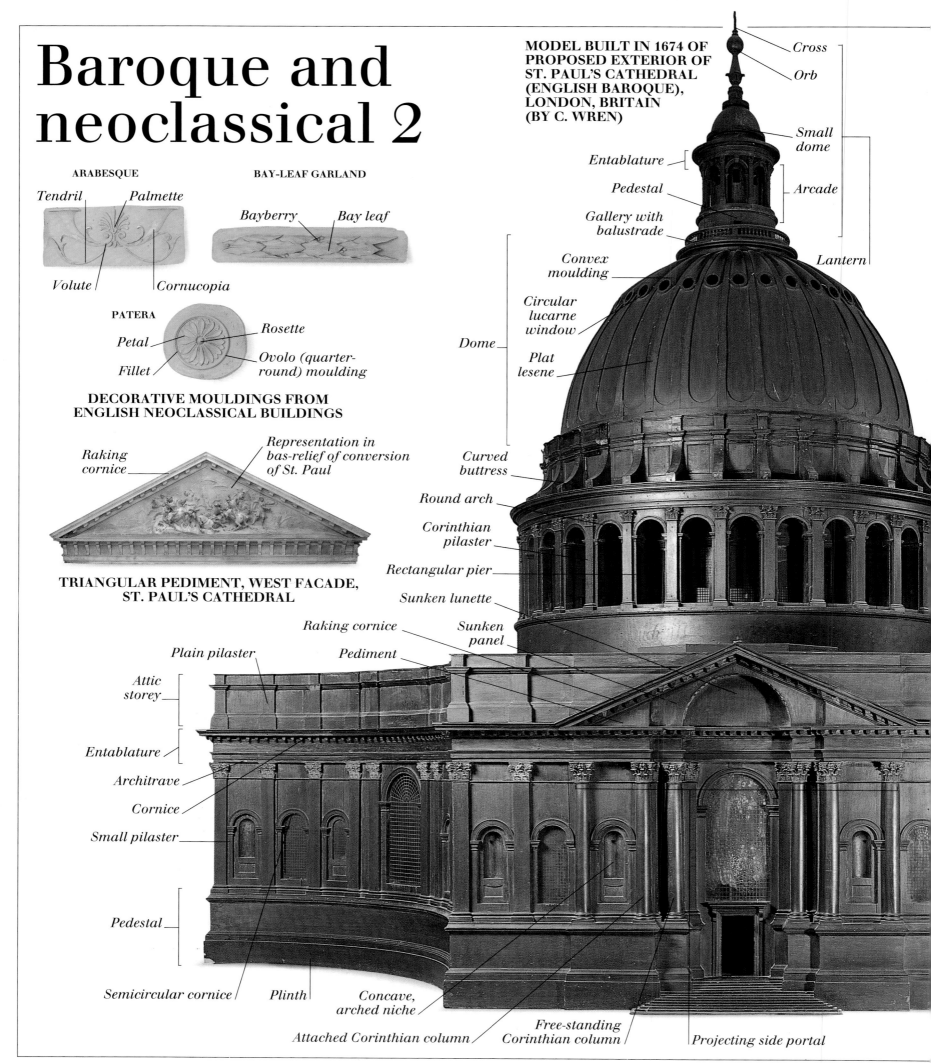

ARABESQUE

Tendril
Palmette
Volute
Cornucopia

BAY-LEAF GARLAND

Bayberry
Bay leaf

PATERA

Petal
Fillet
Rosette
Ovolo (quarter-round) moulding

DECORATIVE MOULDINGS FROM ENGLISH NEOCLASSICAL BUILDINGS

Raking cornice
Representation in bas-relief of conversion of St. Paul

TRIANGULAR PEDIMENT, WEST FACADE, ST. PAUL'S CATHEDRAL

MODEL BUILT IN 1674 OF PROPOSED EXTERIOR OF ST. PAUL'S CATHEDRAL (ENGLISH BAROQUE), LONDON, BRITAIN (BY C. WREN)

Cross
Orb
Small dome
Entablature
Pedestal
Arcade
Gallery with balustrade
Lantern
Convex moulding
Circular lucarne window
Dome
Plat lesene
Curved buttress
Round arch
Corinthian pilaster
Rectangular pier
Sunken lunette
Raking cornice
Sunken panel
Pediment
Plain pilaster
Attic storey
Entablature
Architrave
Cornice
Small pilaster
Pedestal
Semicircular cornice
Plinth
Concave, arched niche
Attached Corinthian column
Free-standing Corinthian column
Projecting side portal

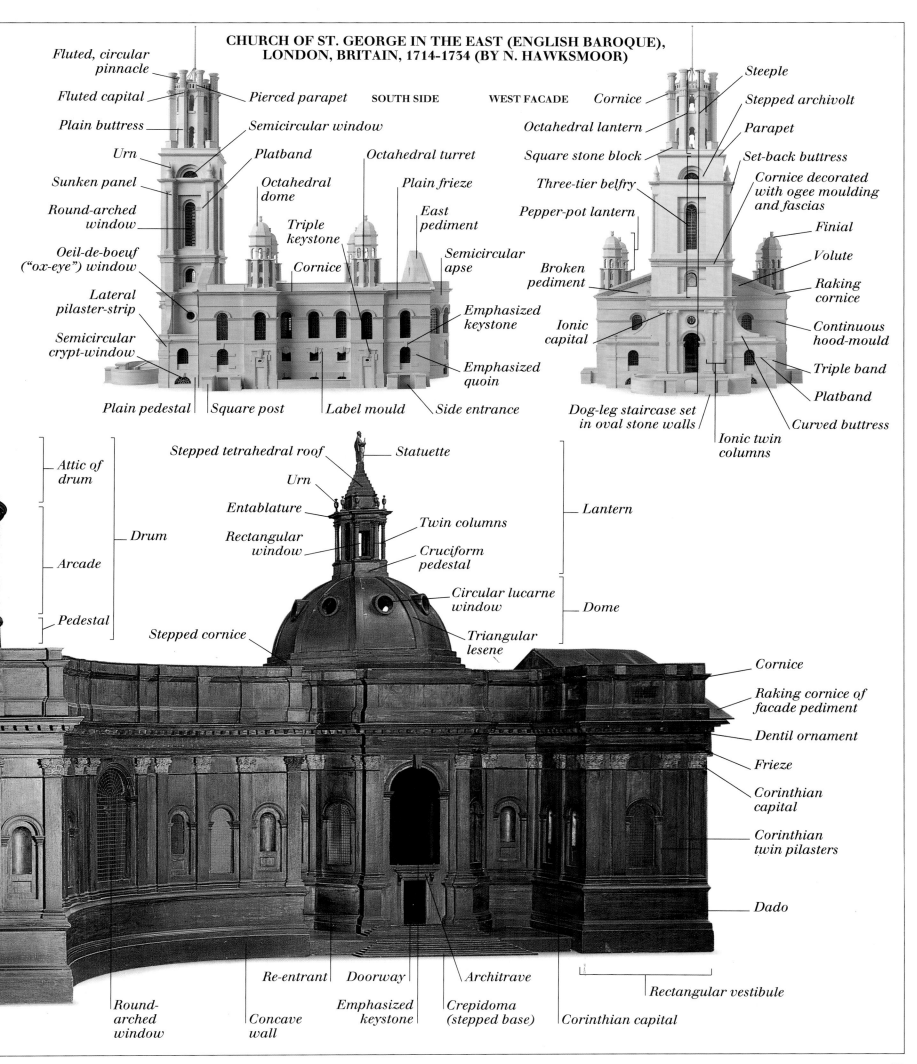

CHURCH OF ST. GEORGE IN THE EAST (ENGLISH BAROQUE), LONDON, BRITAIN, 1714-1734 (BY N. HAWKSMOOR)

SOUTH SIDE　　　WEST FACADE

Fluted, circular pinnacle

Fluted capital

Plain buttress

Urn

Sunken panel

Round-arched window

Oeil-de-boeuf ("ox-eye") window

Lateral pilaster-strip

Semicircular crypt-window

Pierced parapet

Semicircular window

Platband

Octahedral dome

Triple keystone

Cornice

Plain pedestal

Square post

Label mould

Octahedral turret

Plain frieze

East pediment

Semicircular apse

Emphasized keystone

Emphasized quoin

Side entrance

Steeple

Cornice

Octahedral lantern

Square stone block

Three-tier belfry

Pepper-pot lantern

Broken pediment

Ionic capital

Dog-leg staircase set in oval stone walls

Ionic twin columns

Stepped archivolt

Parapet

Set-back buttress

Cornice decorated with ogee moulding and fascias

Finial

Volute

Raking cornice

Continuous hood-mould

Triple band

Platband

Curved buttress

Attic of drum

Drum

Arcade

Pedestal

Stepped tetrahedral roof

Urn

Entablature

Rectangular window

Statuette

Twin columns

Cruciform pedestal

Circular lucarne window

Triangular lesene

Stepped cornice

Lantern

Dome

Cornice

Raking cornice of facade pediment

Dentil ornament

Frieze

Corinthian capital

Corinthian twin pilasters

Dado

Round-arched window

Concave wall

Re-entrant

Doorway

Emphasized keystone

Architrave

Crepidoma (stepped base)

Corinthian capital

Rectangular vestibule

33

Baroque and neoclassical 3

DETAILS FROM BAROQUE, NEOCLASSICAL, AND ROCOCO BUILDINGS

PORTICO, THE VYNE, HAMPSHIRE, BRITAIN, 1654 (NEOCLASSICAL)

GILT IRONWORK FROM SCREEN, PALAIS DE VERSAILLES, FRANCE, 1669-1674 (FRENCH BAROQUE)

WINDOW, PALAZZO STANGA, CREMONA, ITALY, EARLY 18TH CENTURY (ROCOCO)

ATLAS (MALE CARYATID), UPPER BELVEDERE, VIENNA, AUSTRIA, 1721 (GERMAN-STYLE BAROQUE)

BALCONY, NANTES, FRANCE, 1730-1740 (ROCOCO)

MASONRY OF A NICHE IN THE ROTUNDA (NEOCLASSICAL), BANK OF ENGLAND, LONDON, BRITAIN, 1794 (BY J. SOANE)

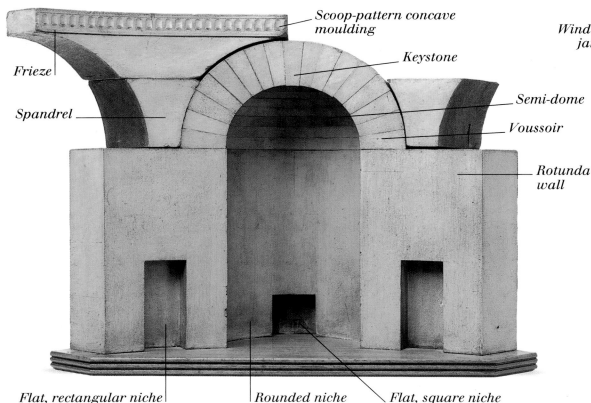

- Scoop-pattern concave moulding
- Keystone
- Frieze
- Spandrel
- Semi-dome
- Voussoir
- Rotunda wall
- Flat, rectangular niche
- Rounded niche
- Flat, square niche

CORNER OF THE NEW STATE PAPER OFFICE (NEOCLASSICAL), LONDON, BRITAIN, 1830-1831 (BY J. SOANE)

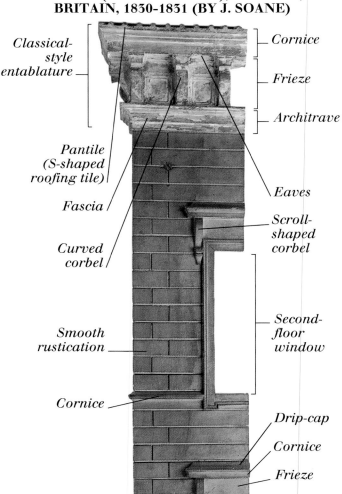
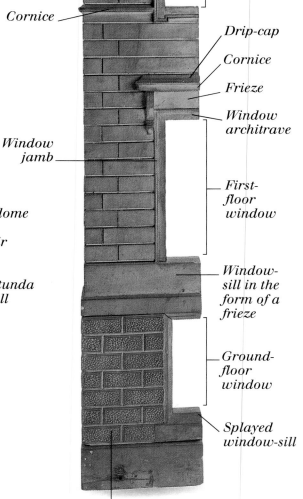

- Classical-style entablature
- Cornice
- Frieze
- Architrave
- Pantile (S-shaped roofing tile)
- Fascia
- Curved corbel
- Eaves
- Scroll-shaped corbel
- Smooth rustication
- Second-floor window
- Cornice
- Drip-cap
- Cornice
- Frieze
- Window architrave
- Window jamb
- First-floor window
- Window-sill in the form of a frieze
- Ground-floor window
- Splayed window-sill
- Vermiculated rustication

TYRINGHAM HOUSE (NEOCLASSICAL), BUCKINGHAMSHIRE, BRITAIN, 1793-1797 (BY J. SOANE)

ROOF LEVEL (ATTIC LEVEL)

Space for illumination above unroofed central hall

Chimney-stack

Space above unroofed main staircase

Flat roof

Oculus illuminating secondary staircase

Parapet rail

Balustrade

Baluster

Cornice

Attic storey of convex portico

Cornice

FIRST-FLOOR LEVEL (CHAMBER FLOOR)

Upper level of central hall, open to floor below

Main staircase

Secondary staircase

Abacus

Triangular pilaster

Pilaster capital

First-floor storey of convex portico

Attached Tuscan twin pilasters

Window-sill

Bow front

GROUND-FLOOR LEVEL (PRINCIPAL FLOOR)

Withdrawing-room

Central hall

Library and breakfast-room

Main staircase

Water-closet (toilet)

Eating-room

Secondary staircase

Segmented lintel course

Band incised with Greek-style fret ornament

Window-sill

Window architrave

Window jamb

Base

Basement

Plinth

Horizontal rustication

Vestibule (entrance hall)

Ground-floor storey of convex portico

FACADE OF TYRINGHAM HOUSE

Chimney-stack

Voussoir

Basement window

Entrance door

Circular entrance steps

Baluster

Rail

Balustrade

Parapet

Entablature

Cornice

Capital

Shaft

Ionic column

Base

PROSTYLE COLONNADE

Ceilings

EARLY CEILINGS WERE SIMPLY the underside of the floor above, with the timbers exposed. By the 16th century the timbers were covered with boards and stucco (plaster). Moulded stucco ceilings became popular in the 17th century; some of them were elaborately ornamented, such as the one shown here. Even today, board-and-plaster ceilings are commonly used in new buildings.

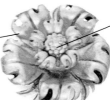

Scrolled petal

Stylized stamen

PATERA (ROSETTE)

MOULDED STUCCO CEILING, THE BANQUETING HOUSE, WHITEHALL PALACE, LONDON, BRITAIN, 1666-1693 (DESIGNED BY I. JONES, PAINTED BY P.P. RUBENS)

MIDDLE PANELS: TRIUMPHAL PROCESSION OF CHERUBS (TOP AND BOTTOM); GLORIFICATION OF JAMES I (CENTRE)

TOP-LEFT PANEL: HERCULES CHASTISES ENVY

Figure symbolizing envy (rebellion)

Hercules symbolizing strength

Acanthus leaf

Patera (rosette)

CENTRE-LEFT PANEL: UNION OF THE KINGDOMS OF ENGLAND AND SCOTLAND

Figure symbolizing Scotland

Child symbolizing the union of Scotland and England

Figure symbolizing England

Britannia (symbolizing Britain) in the guise of Minerva (goddess of wisdom)

James I (King of England and Scotland)

BOTTOM-LEFT PANEL: MINERVA STRIKES DOWN IGNORANCE

Sunken panel

Small panel

Modillion (bracket)

Figure symbolizing ignorance

Minerva (goddess of wisdom)

Arabesque

Laurel wreath symbolizing victory

Symbol of Mercury (messenger of the gods)

DETAILS OF MOULDED STUCCO FROM THE BANQUETING HOUSE CEILING

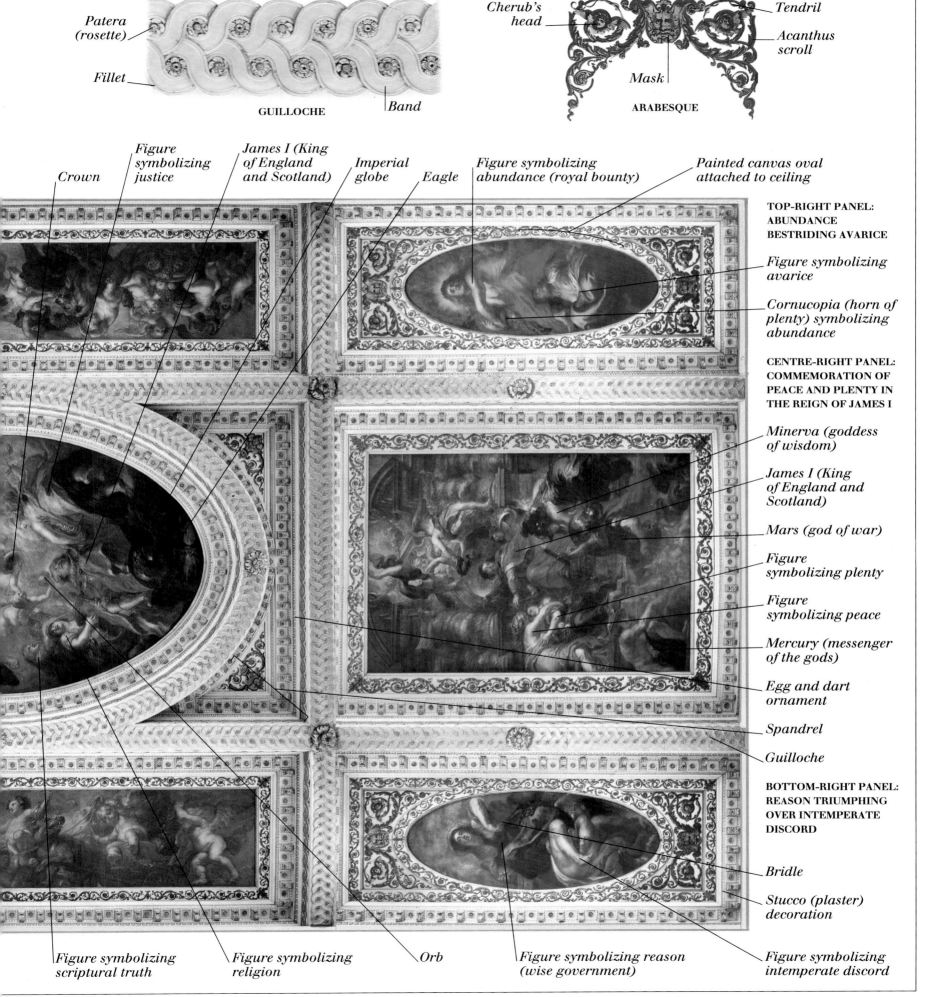

Patera (rosette)

Fillet

GUILLOCHE

Band

Cherub's head

Tendril

Acanthus scroll

Mask

ARABESQUE

Crown

Figure symbolizing justice

James I (King of England and Scotland)

Imperial globe

Eagle

Figure symbolizing abundance (royal bounty)

Painted canvas oval attached to ceiling

TOP-RIGHT PANEL: ABUNDANCE BESTRIDING AVARICE

Figure symbolizing avarice

Cornucopia (horn of plenty) symbolizing abundance

CENTRE-RIGHT PANEL: COMMEMORATION OF PEACE AND PLENTY IN THE REIGN OF JAMES I

Minerva (goddess of wisdom)

James I (King of England and Scotland)

Mars (god of war)

Figure symbolizing plenty

Figure symbolizing peace

Mercury (messenger of the gods)

Egg and dart ornament

Spandrel

Guilloche

BOTTOM-RIGHT PANEL: REASON TRIUMPHING OVER INTEMPERATE DISCORD

Bridle

Stucco (plaster) decoration

Figure symbolizing scriptural truth

Figure symbolizing religion

Orb

Figure symbolizing reason (wise government)

Figure symbolizing intemperate discord

Arches and vaults

ARCHES ARE CURVED STRUCTURES used to bridge spans and to support the weight of upper parts of buildings, such as domes, as in St. Paul's Cathedral (below) and the antique temple (opposite). The voussoirs (wedge-shaped blocks) that form an arch (right) support each other and convert the downward force of the weight of the building into an outward force. This outward force is in turn transferred to buttresses, piers, or abutments. A vault is an arched roof or ceiling. There are four main types of vault (opposite). A barrel vault is a single vault, semicircular in cross-section; a groin vault consists of two barrel vaults intersecting at right-angles; a rib vault is a groin vault reinforced by ribs; and a fan vault is a rib vault in which the ribs radiate from the springing point (where the arch begins) like a fan.

PARTS OF AN ARCH

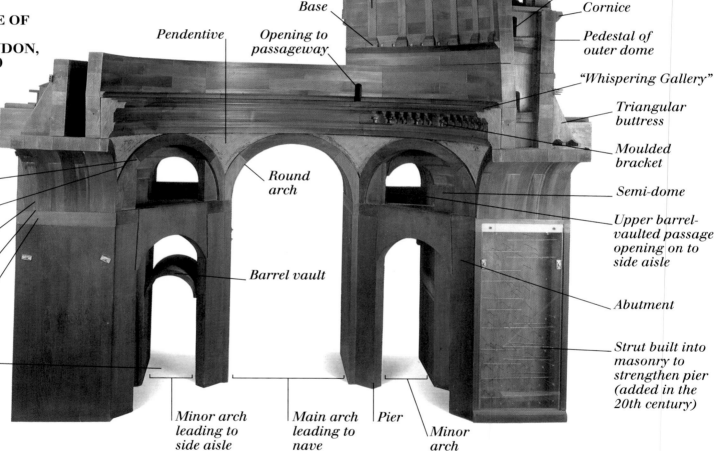

Voussoir   Keystone   Crown   Abutment

Keystone

Abutment

Extrados

Intrados (soffit)   Haunch

Impost

Intrados (soffit)

Springing point

Abutment

Span

Abutment

FRONT   **SIDE**

ARCHES AND BASE OF DOME, ST. PAUL'S CATHEDRAL, LONDON, BRITAIN, 1675-1710 (BY C. WREN)

Inner dome   Colonnade

Pilaster   Passageway

Base   Cornice

Pendentive   Opening to passageway   Pedestal of outer dome

"Whispering Gallery"

Upper arch (concealing difference in heights between main arch and minor arches)   Triangular buttress

Moulded bracket

Round arch

Semi-dome

Extrados

Intrados (soffit)   Upper barrel-vaulted passage opening on to side aisle

Springing point

Impost   Abutment

Barrel vault

Passage leading to side aisle   Strut built into masonry to strengthen pier (added in the 20th century)

Minor arch leading to side aisle   Main arch leading to nave   Pier   Minor arch

TYPES OF ARCH

HORSESHOE ARCH (MOORISH ARCH), GREAT MOSQUE, CORDOBA, SPAIN, 785

BASKET ARCH (SEMI-ELLIPTICAL ARCH), PALATINE CHAPEL, AIX-LA-CHAPELLE, FRANCE, 790-798

TUDOR ARCH, TOWER OF LONDON, BRITAIN, c.1086-1097

LANCET ARCH, WESTMINSTER ABBEY, LONDON, BRITAIN, 1503-1519

TREFOIL ARCH, BEVERLEY MINSTER, YORKSHIRE, BRITAIN, c.1300

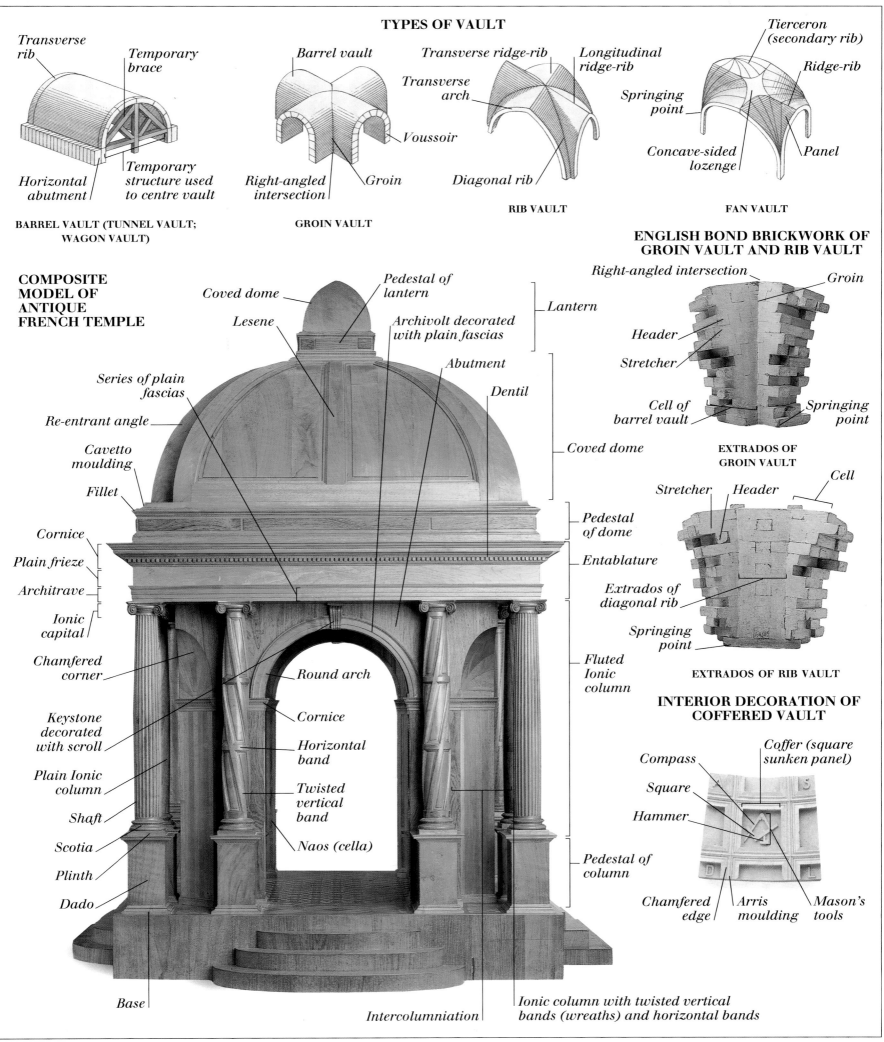

TYPES OF VAULT

Transverse rib
Temporary brace
Horizontal abutment
Temporary structure used to centre vault

BARREL VAULT (TUNNEL VAULT; WAGON VAULT)

Barrel vault
Right-angled intersection
Groin
Voussoir

GROIN VAULT

Transverse ridge-rib
Longitudinal ridge-rib
Transverse arch
Diagonal rib

RIB VAULT

Tierceron (secondary rib)
Ridge-rib
Springing point
Concave-sided lozenge
Panel

FAN VAULT

COMPOSITE MODEL OF ANTIQUE FRENCH TEMPLE

Coved dome
Pedestal of lantern
Lesene
Archivolt decorated with plain fascias
Lantern
Series of plain fascias
Abutment
Re-entrant angle
Dentil
Cavetto moulding
Coved dome
Fillet
Pedestal of dome
Cornice
Entablature
Plain frieze
Architrave
Ionic capital
Fluted Ionic column
Chamfered corner
Round arch
Keystone decorated with scroll
Cornice
Horizontal band
Plain Ionic column
Twisted vertical band
Shaft
Naos (cella)
Scotia
Plinth
Dado
Pedestal of column
Base
Intercolumniation
Ionic column with twisted vertical bands (wreaths) and horizontal bands

ENGLISH BOND BRICKWORK OF GROIN VAULT AND RIB VAULT

Right-angled intersection
Groin
Header
Stretcher
Cell of barrel vault
Springing point

EXTRADOS OF GROIN VAULT

Stretcher
Header
Cell
Extrados of diagonal rib
Springing point

EXTRADOS OF RIB VAULT

INTERIOR DECORATION OF COFFERED VAULT

Compass
Coffer (square sunken panel)
Square
Hammer
Chamfered edge
Arris moulding
Mason's tools

Domes

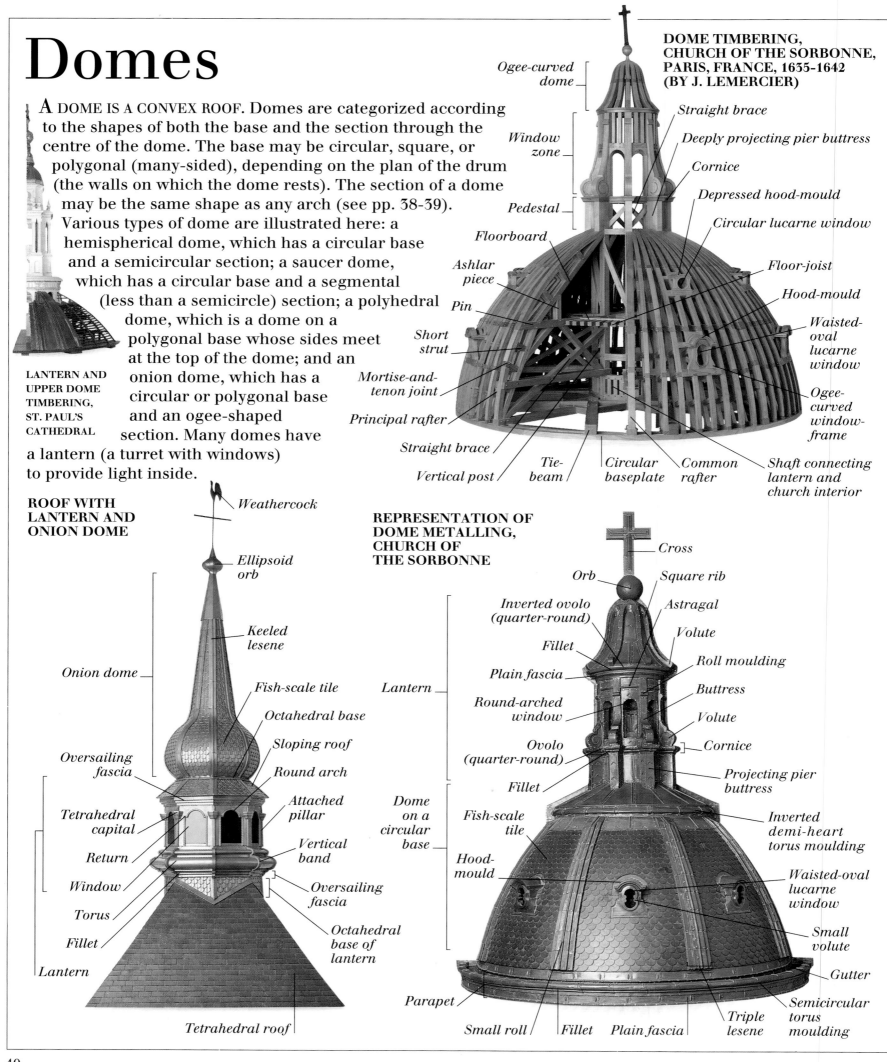

A DOME IS A CONVEX ROOF. Domes are categorized according to the shapes of both the base and the section through the centre of the dome. The base may be circular, square, or polygonal (many-sided), depending on the plan of the drum (the walls on which the dome rests). The section of a dome may be the same shape as any arch (see pp. 38-39). Various types of dome are illustrated here: a hemispherical dome, which has a circular base and a semicircular section; a saucer dome, which has a circular base and a segmental (less than a semicircle) section; a polyhedral dome, which is a dome on a polygonal base whose sides meet at the top of the dome; and an onion dome, which has a circular or polygonal base and an ogee-shaped section. Many domes have a lantern (a turret with windows) to provide light inside.

LANTERN AND UPPER DOME TIMBERING, ST. PAUL'S CATHEDRAL

DOME TIMBERING, CHURCH OF THE SORBONNE, PARIS, FRANCE, 1635-1642 (BY J. LEMERCIER)

Ogee-curved dome
Window zone
Pedestal
Floorboard
Ashlar piece
Pin
Short strut
Mortise-and-tenon joint
Principal rafter
Straight brace
Vertical post
Tie-beam
Circular baseplate
Common rafter
Straight brace
Deeply projecting pier buttress
Cornice
Depressed hood-mould
Circular lucarne window
Floor-joist
Hood-mould
Waisted-oval lucarne window
Ogee-curved window-frame
Shaft connecting lantern and church interior

ROOF WITH LANTERN AND ONION DOME

Weathercock
Ellipsoid orb
Keeled lesene
Onion dome
Fish-scale tile
Octahedral base
Oversailing fascia
Sloping roof
Round arch
Tetrahedral capital
Attached pillar
Return
Vertical band
Window
Oversailing fascia
Torus
Octahedral base of lantern
Fillet
Lantern
Tetrahedral roof

REPRESENTATION OF DOME METALLING, CHURCH OF THE SORBONNE

Cross
Orb
Square rib
Inverted ovolo (quarter-round)
Astragal
Volute
Fillet
Roll moulding
Plain fascia
Buttress
Lantern
Round-arched window
Volute
Ovolo (quarter-round)
Cornice
Fillet
Projecting pier buttress
Dome on a circular base
Fish-scale tile
Inverted demi-heart torus moulding
Hood-mould
Waisted-oval lucarne window
Small volute
Gutter
Parapet
Semicircular torus moulding
Small roll
Fillet
Plain fascia
Triple lesene

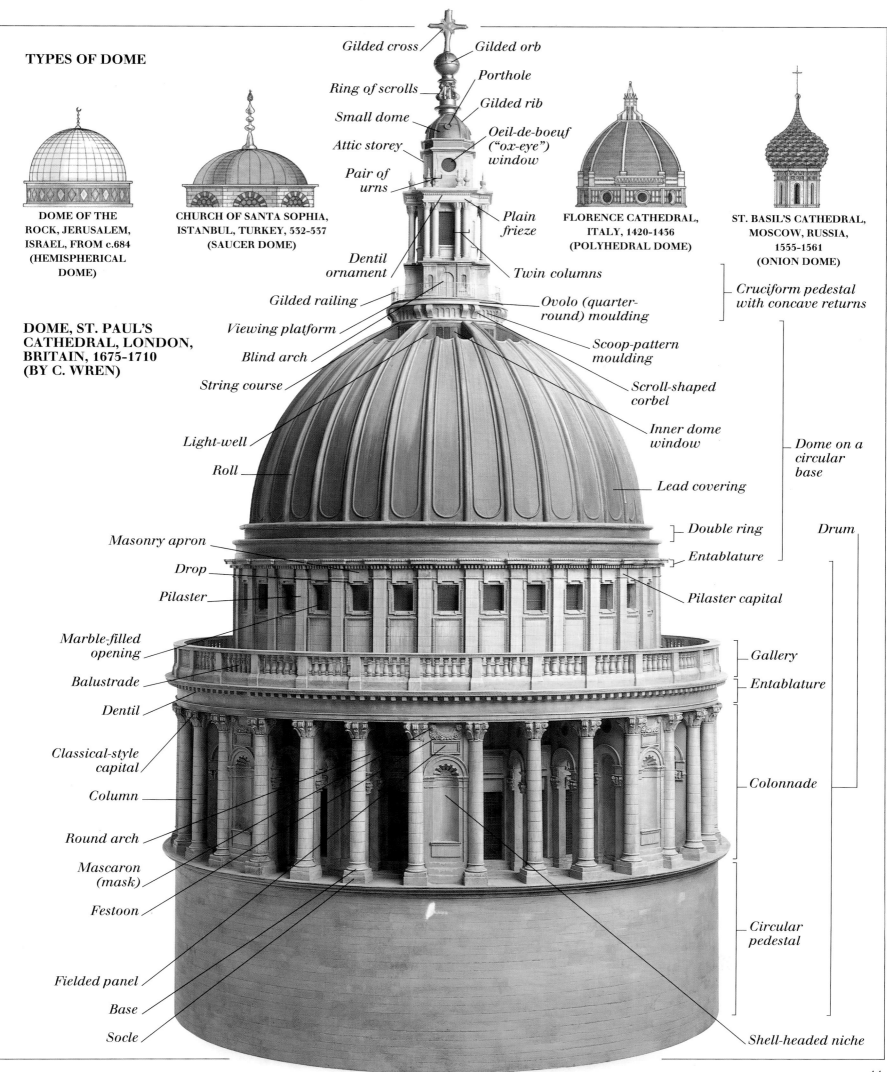

TYPES OF DOME

DOME OF THE
ROCK, JERUSALEM,
ISRAEL, FROM c.684
(HEMISPHERICAL
DOME)

CHURCH OF SANTA SOPHIA,
ISTANBUL, TURKEY, 532-537
(SAUCER DOME)

FLORENCE CATHEDRAL,
ITALY, 1420-1436
(POLYHEDRAL DOME)

ST. BASIL'S CATHEDRAL,
MOSCOW, RUSSIA,
1555-1561
(ONION DOME)

**DOME, ST. PAUL'S
CATHEDRAL, LONDON,
BRITAIN, 1675-1710
(BY C. WREN)**

Gilded cross

Gilded orb

Ring of scrolls

Porthole

Small dome

Gilded rib

Attic storey

Oeil-de-boeuf
("ox-eye")
window

Pair of
urns

Plain
frieze

Dentil
ornament

Twin columns

Gilded railing

Ovolo (quarter-
round) moulding

Viewing platform

Scoop-pattern
moulding

Blind arch

Scroll-shaped
corbel

String course

Inner dome
window

Light-well

Lead covering

Roll

Double ring

Masonry apron

Entablature

Drop

Pilaster

Pilaster capital

Marble-filled
opening

Gallery

Balustrade

Entablature

Dentil

Classical-style
capital

Colonnade

Column

Round arch

Mascaron
(mask)

Festoon

Fielded panel

Base

Socle

Shell-headed niche

Cruciform pedestal
with concave returns

Dome on a
circular
base

Drum

Circular
pedestal

41

Islamic buildings

OPUS SECTILE MOSAIC DESIGN

THE ISLAMIC RELIGION was founded by the prophet Mohammed, who was born in Mecca (in present-day Saudi Arabia) about 570 AD. In the following three centuries, Islam spread from Arabia to North Africa and Spain, as well as to India and much of the rest of Asia. The worldwide influence of Islam remains strong today. Common characteristics of Islamic buildings include ogee arches and roofs, onion domes, and walls decorated with carved stone, paintings, inlays, or mosaics. The most important type of Islamic building is the mosque – the place of worship – which generally has a minaret (tower) from which the muezzin (official crier) calls Muslims to prayer. Most mosques have a mihrab (decorative niche) that indicates the direction of Mecca. As figurative art is not allowed in Islam, buildings are ornamented with geometric and arabesque motifs, and inscriptions (frequently Koranic verses).

Bud-like onion dome

Depressed arch surrounding mihrab

Painted roof pavilion

Lotus-flower pendentive

Turkish-crescent finial

Arabic inscription

Crest

Painted minaret with censer (incense burner)

Spandrel

Series of recessed arches

Semi-dome

Arched niche within a niche

Mural resembling tomb

Polyhedral niche

Recessed colonettes

MIHRAB, JAMI MASJID (PRINCIPAL OR CONGREGATIONAL MOSQUE), BIJAPUR, INDIA, c.1636

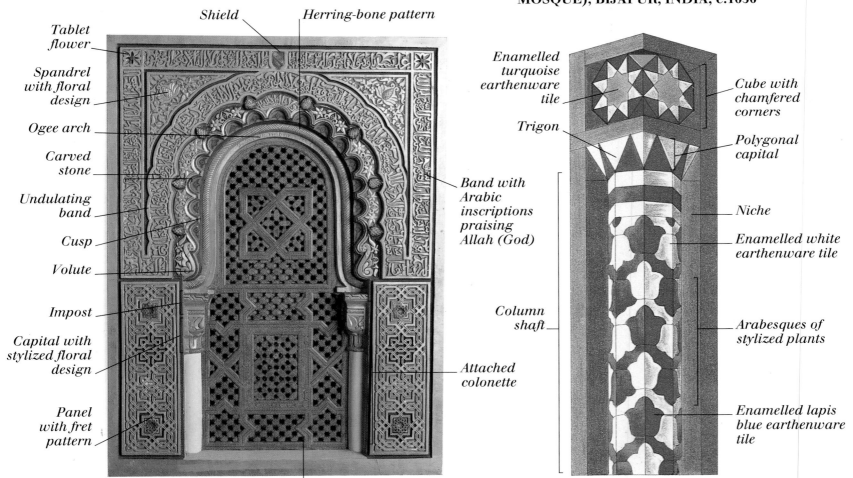

Shield

Herring-bone pattern

Tablet flower

Spandrel with floral design

Ogee arch

Carved stone

Undulating band

Cusp

Volute

Impost

Capital with stylized floral design

Panel with fret pattern

Band with Arabic inscriptions praising Allah (God)

Attached colonette

Jali (latticed screen) with geometrical patterns

ARCH, THE ALHAMBRA, GRANADA, SPAIN, 1333-1354

Enamelled turquoise earthenware tile

Cube with chamfered corners

Trigon

Polygonal capital

Niche

Enamelled white earthenware tile

Column shaft

Arabesques of stylized plants

Enamelled lapis blue earthenware tile

MIHRAB WITH COLUMN, EL-AINYI MOSQUE, CAIRO, EGYPT, 15TH CENTURY

EXAMPLES OF ISLAMIC MOSAICS, EGYPT AND SYRIA

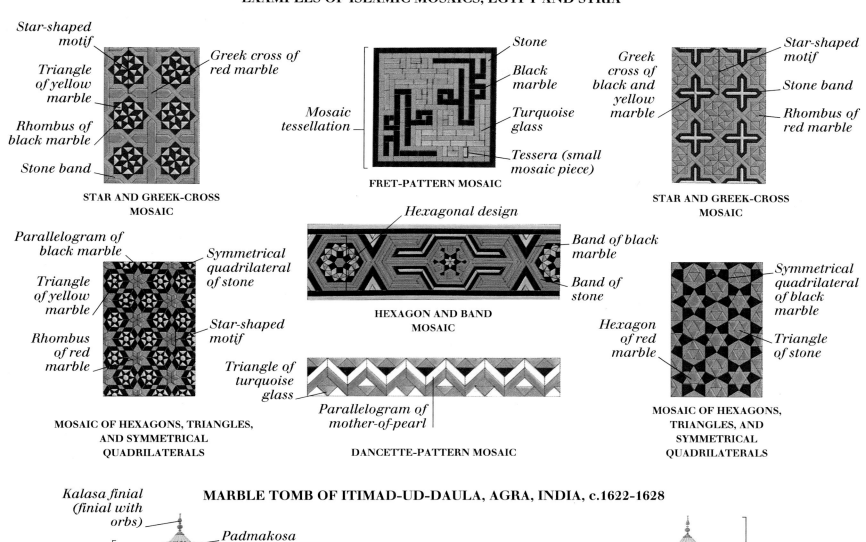

Star-shaped motif
Triangle of yellow marble
Greek cross of red marble
Rhombus of black marble
Stone band

STAR AND GREEK-CROSS MOSAIC

Mosaic tessellation
Stone
Black marble
Turquoise glass
Tessera (small mosaic piece)

FRET-PATTERN MOSAIC

Greek cross of black and yellow marble
Star-shaped motif
Stone band
Rhombus of red marble

STAR AND GREEK-CROSS MOSAIC

Parallelogram of black marble
Symmetrical quadrilateral of stone
Triangle of yellow marble
Star-shaped motif
Rhombus of red marble

MOSAIC OF HEXAGONS, TRIANGLES, AND SYMMETRICAL QUADRILATERALS

Hexagonal design
Band of black marble
Band of stone

HEXAGON AND BAND MOSAIC

Triangle of turquoise glass
Parallelogram of mother-of-pearl

DANCETTE-PATTERN MOSAIC

Symmetrical quadrilateral of black marble
Hexagon of red marble
Triangle of stone

MOSAIC OF HEXAGONS, TRIANGLES, AND SYMMETRICAL QUADRILATERALS

MARBLE TOMB OF ITIMAD-UD-DAULA, AGRA, INDIA, c.1622-1628

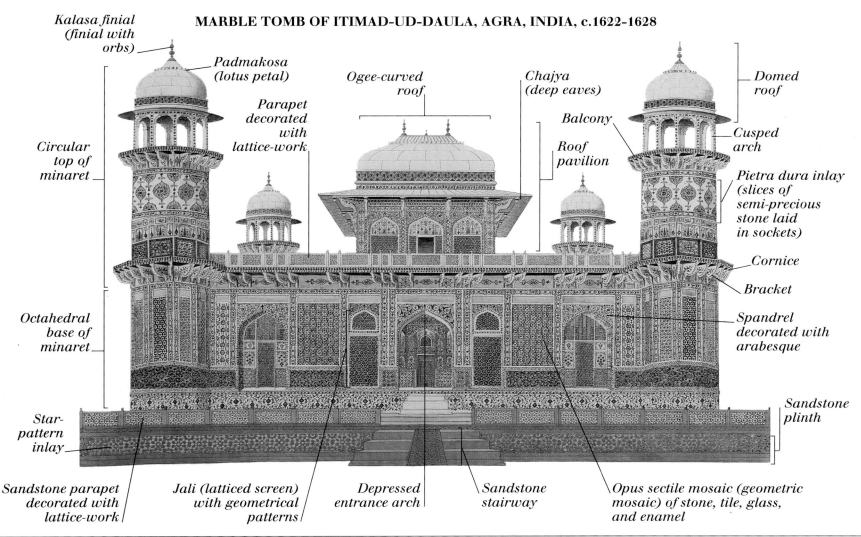

Kalasa finial (finial with orbs)
Padmakosa (lotus petal)
Ogee-curved roof
Chajya (deep eaves)
Domed roof
Parapet decorated with lattice-work
Balcony
Cusped arch
Circular top of minaret
Roof pavilion
Pietra dura inlay (slices of semi-precious stone laid in sockets)
Cornice
Bracket
Octahedral base of minaret
Spandrel decorated with arabesque
Star-pattern inlay
Sandstone plinth
Sandstone parapet decorated with lattice-work
Jali (latticed screen) with geometrical patterns
Depressed entrance arch
Sandstone stairway
Opus sectile mosaic (geometric mosaic) of stone, tile, glass, and enamel

South and east Asia

THE TRADITIONAL ARCHITECTURE of south and east Asia has been profoundly influenced by the spread from India of Buddhism and Hinduism. This influence is shown both by the abundance and by the architectural styles of temples and shrines in the region. Many early Hindu temples consist of rooms carved from solid rock-faces. However, free-standing structures began to be built in southern India from about the eighth century AD. Many were built in the Dravidian style, like the Temple of Virupaksha (opposite) with its characteristic antarala (terraced tower), perforated windows, and numerous arches, pilasters, and carvings. The earliest Buddhist religious monuments were Indian stupas (see pp. 58-59), which consisted of a single hemispherical dome surmounted by a chattravali (shaft) and surrounded by railings with ornate gates. Later Indian stupas and those built elsewhere were sometimes modified; for example, in Sri Lanka, the dome became bell-shaped, and was called a dagoba. Buddhist pagodas, such as the Burmese example (right), are multistoreyed temples, each storey having a projecting roof. The form of these buildings probably derived from the yasti (pointed spire) of the stupa. Another feature of many traditional Asian buildings is their imaginative roof-forms, such as gambrel (mansard) roofs, and roofs with angle-rafters (below).

SEVEN-STOREYED PAGODA IN BURMESE STYLE, c.9TH-10TH CENTURY

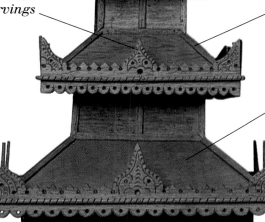

Gilded band

Gilded iron hti (crown)

Dubika (mast)

Arrow motif

Torus moulding with spiral carving

Decorative eaves board

Ogee-arched motif with decorative carvings

Ogee-arched motif forming horn

Hip-rafter

Pentroof

Undulating moulding

Baluster finial

Balustrade

Pillar

Engaged pillar

Arched entrance

Rectangular window

Baluster

Straight brace

DETAILS FROM EAST ASIAN BUILDINGS

KASUGA-STYLE ROOF WITH SUMIGI (ANGLE-RAFTERS), KASUGADO SHRINE OF ENJOJI, NARA, JAPAN, 12TH-14TH CENTURY

TERRACES, TEMPLE OF HEAVEN, BEIJING, CHINA, 15TH CENTURY

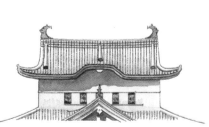

GAMBREL (MANSARD) ROOF WITH UPSWEPT EAVES AND UNDULATING GABLES, HIMEJI CASTLE, HIMEJI, JAPAN, 1608-1609

CORNER CAPITAL WITH ROOF BEAMS, POPCHU-SA TEMPLE, POPCHU-SA, SOUTH KOREA, 17TH CENTURY

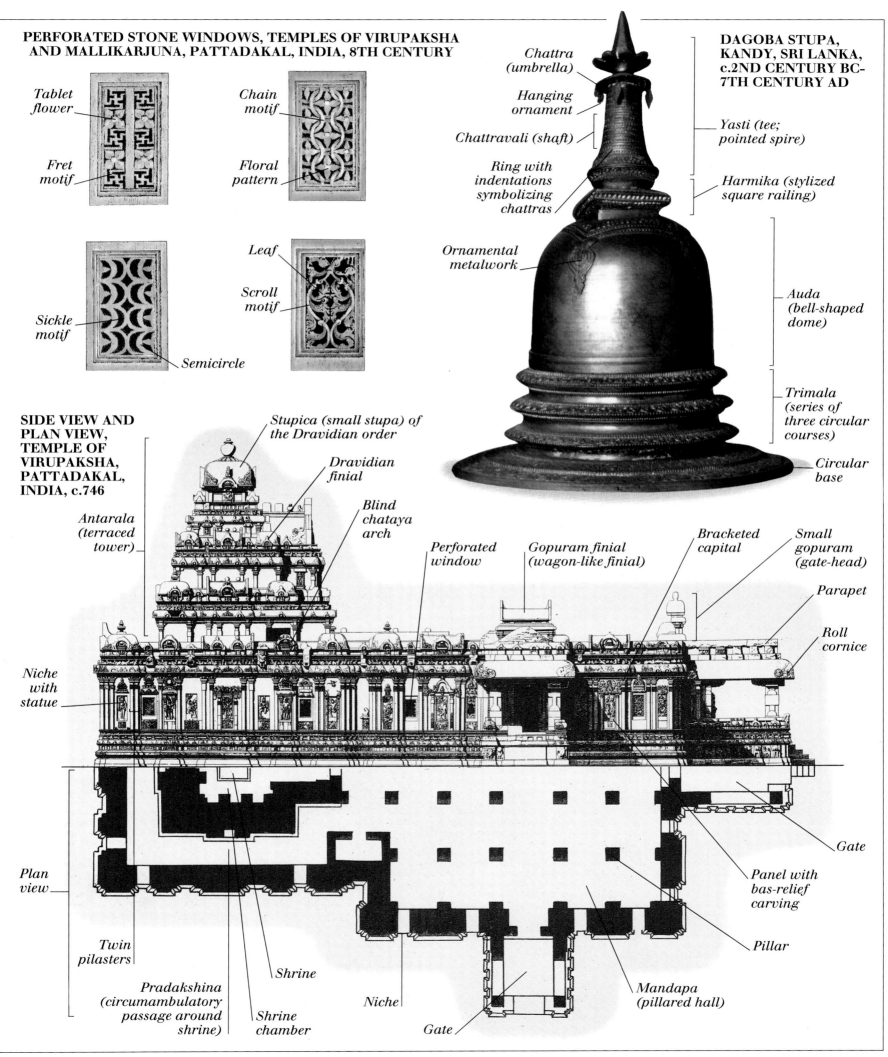

PERFORATED STONE WINDOWS, TEMPLES OF VIRUPAKSHA AND MALLIKARJUNA, PATTADAKAL, INDIA, 8TH CENTURY

Tablet flower

Fret motif

Chain motif

Floral pattern

Sickle motif

Semicircle

Leaf

Scroll motif

DAGOBA STUPA, KANDY, SRI LANKA, c.2ND CENTURY BC-7TH CENTURY AD

Chattra (umbrella)

Hanging ornament

Chattravali (shaft)

Ring with indentations symbolizing chattras

Ornamental metalwork

Yasti (tee; pointed spire)

Harmika (stylized square railing)

Auda (bell-shaped dome)

Trimala (series of three circular courses)

Circular base

SIDE VIEW AND PLAN VIEW, TEMPLE OF VIRUPAKSHA, PATTADAKAL, INDIA, c.746

Stupica (small stupa) of the Dravidian order

Dravidian finial

Blind chataya arch

Antarala (terraced tower)

Perforated window

Gopuram finial (wagon-like finial)

Bracketed capital

Small gopuram (gate-head)

Parapet

Roll cornice

Niche with statue

Gate

Panel with bas-relief carving

Plan view

Pillar

Twin pilasters

Shrine

Pradakshina (circumambulatory passage around shrine)

Shrine chamber

Niche

Gate

Mandapa (pillared hall)

45

Doors

A DOOR AND ITS SURROUNDING FRAME make up a doorway. Doorways that are particularly grand or imposing are known as portals, examples of which include the portals of Lund and Cologne Cathedrals (opposite). There are two main types of door, panelled and matchboarded, both of which were used as long ago as ancient Egyptian times. Panelled doors consist of a frame of horizontal rails and vertical muntins, with infill panels of wood or glass. Matchboarded doors consist of long, vertical boards held in position by horizontal rails and diagonal braces.

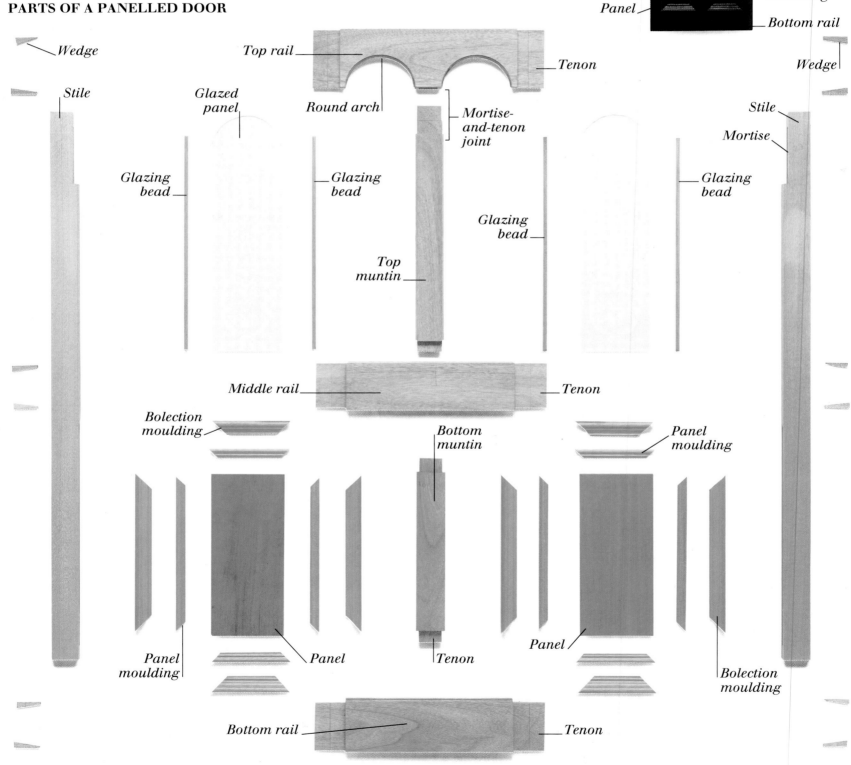

PARTS OF A PANELLED DOOR

TYPES OF DOOR

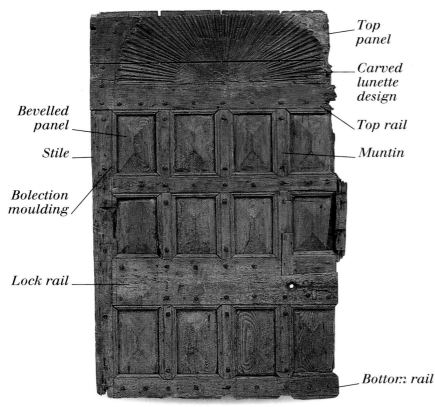

Top panel

Carved lunette design

Top rail

Bevelled panel

Stile

Muntin

Bolection moulding

Lock rail

Bottom rail

PANELLED EXTERNAL DOOR, HOUSE, SURREY, BRITAIN, c.1625-1630

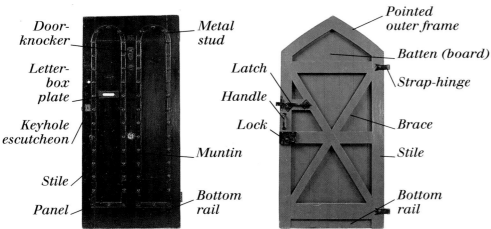

Door-knocker

Metal stud

Letter-box plate

Pointed outer frame

Batten (board)

Latch

Strap-hinge

Handle

Keyhole escutcheon

Lock

Brace

Muntin

Stile

Stile

Bottom rail

Panel

Bottom rail

TWIN-PANELLED FRONT DOOR, HOUSE, LONDON, BRITAIN, c.1830

GOTHIC-STYLE EXTERNAL MATCHBOARDED DOOR, RIPLEY CHURCH SCHOOL, BRITAIN, c.1846

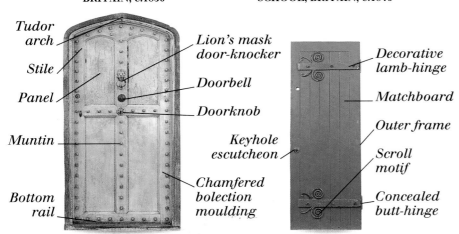

Tudor arch

Lion's mask door-knocker

Stile

Doorbell

Panel

Doorknob

Muntin

Keyhole escutcheon

Bottom rail

Chamfered bolection moulding

Decorative lamb-hinge

Matchboard

Outer frame

Scroll motif

Concealed butt-hinge

TUDOR-STYLE FOUR-PANELLED FRONT DOOR, VILLA, GODALMING, BRITAIN, c.1859

MATCHBOARDED DOOR OF INTERNAL STAIRCASE, RAINHILL ASYLUM, BRITAIN, c.1884

TYPES OF DOORWAY AND PORTAL

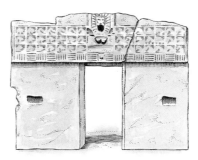

THE GATE OF THE SUN, TIAHUANACO, BOLIVIA, c.600-1000

ANGLO-SAXON TRIANGULAR-ARCHED DOORWAY, BRITAIN, c.900

IONIC DOORWAY, THE ERECHTHEION, ATHENS, GREECE, 421-405 BC

ROMANESQUE PORTAL, LUND CATHEDRAL, SWEDEN, FROM c.1103

GOTHIC PORTAL, COLOGNE CATHEDRAL, GERMANY, FROM 1248

RENAISSANCE DOORWAY, CHURCH OF ST. ZACCARIA, VENICE, ITALY, FROM 1483

ART NOUVEAU ELLIPSOID DOORWAY, PALAU GÜELL, BARCELONA, SPAIN, 1885-1889

ART DECO LIFT DOORWAY, CHRYSLER BUILDING, NEW YORK, USA, 1928-1930

Windows

OEIL-DE-BOEUF ("OX-EYE") WINDOW

THE EARLIEST windows were simply openings for light and ventilation. Glazed windows were first used by the ancient Romans, but they did not appear often in domestic houses until about the 16th century. Early glazing consisted of quarrels (small panes of glass) held together by cames (lead strips) to form a light. As windows became larger, the individual lights were joined together by horizontal transoms and vertical mullions. Casement-windows and sash-windows originated in the 16th and 17th centuries. A casement-window can be swung open on a hinge attached to the side of the window-frame, whereas a sash-window slides up and down on a sash-cord attached, via a pulley, to a weight. The development of metal frames – as in the Bauhaus windows at Dessau – and the availability of large panes of glass eventually made it possible to construct buildings almost entirely from glass.

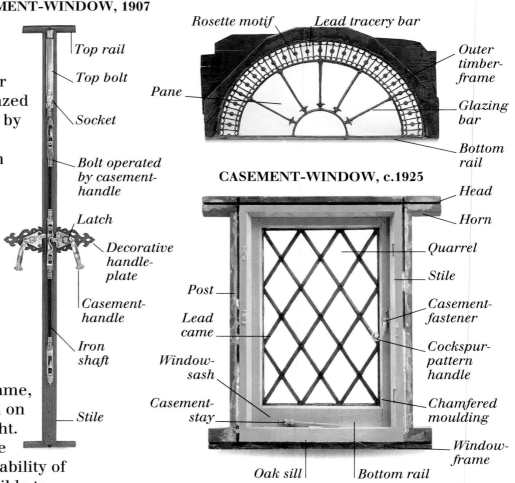

SECTION FROM STEEL CASEMENT-WINDOW, 1907

- Top rail
- Top bolt
- Socket
- Bolt operated by casement-handle
- Latch
- Decorative handle-plate
- Casement-handle
- Iron shaft
- Stile

FANLIGHT, c.1700

- Rosette motif
- Lead tracery bar
- Outer timber-frame
- Pane
- Glazing bar
- Bottom rail

CASEMENT-WINDOW, c.1925

- Head
- Horn
- Quarrel
- Stile
- Casement-fastener
- Cockspur-pattern handle
- Chamfered moulding
- Window-frame
- Bottom rail
- Oak sill
- Casement-stay
- Window-sash
- Lead came
- Post

STAINED GLASS (DETAILS) FROM THE ROYAL COURTS OF JUSTICE, LONDON, BRITAIN, 1866

- Coat of arms
- Lead came
- Quarrel
- Circular quarrel
- Diaper work (background design)
- Rectangular quarrel

VICTORIAN WINDOW WITH SEGMENTAL HEAD, c.1899

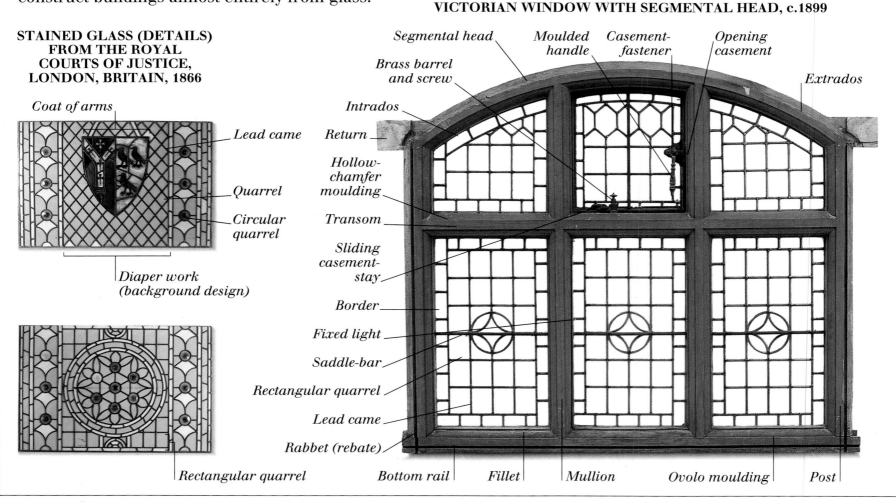

- Segmental head
- Moulded handle
- Casement-fastener
- Opening casement
- Brass barrel and screw
- Extrados
- Intrados
- Return
- Hollow-chamfer moulding
- Transom
- Sliding casement-stay
- Border
- Fixed light
- Saddle-bar
- Rectangular quarrel
- Lead came
- Rabbet (rebate)
- Bottom rail
- Fillet
- Mullion
- Ovolo moulding
- Post

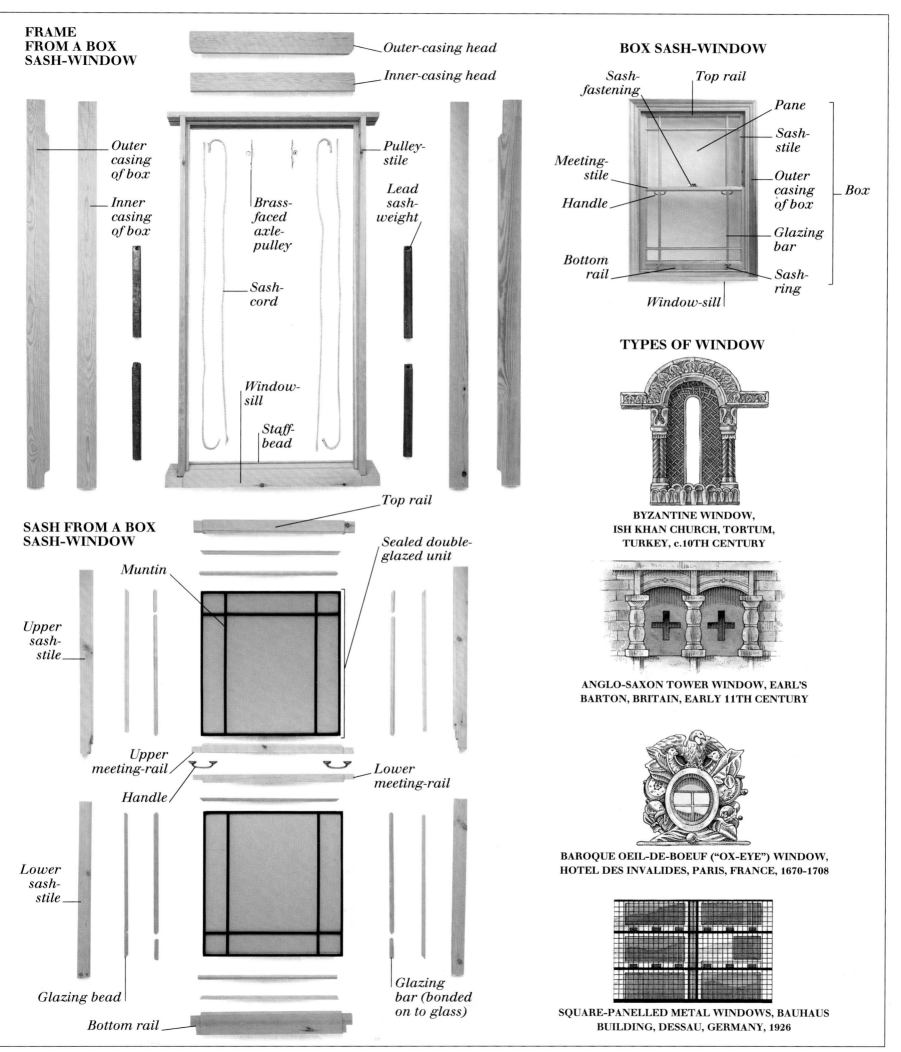

FRAME FROM A BOX SASH-WINDOW

Outer-casing head

Inner-casing head

Outer casing of box

Inner casing of box

Pulley-stile

Brass-faced axle-pulley

Lead sash-weight

Sash-cord

Window-sill

Staff-bead

SASH FROM A BOX SASH-WINDOW

Top rail

Muntin

Sealed double-glazed unit

Upper sash-stile

Lower sash-stile

Upper meeting-rail

Lower meeting-rail

Handle

Glazing bead

Glazing bar (bonded on to glass)

Bottom rail

BOX SASH-WINDOW

Sash-fastening

Top rail

Pane

Sash-stile

Meeting-stile

Handle

Outer casing of box

Box

Bottom rail

Glazing bar

Sash-ring

Window-sill

TYPES OF WINDOW

**BYZANTINE WINDOW,
ISH KHAN CHURCH, TORTUM,
TURKEY, c.10TH CENTURY**

**ANGLO-SAXON TOWER WINDOW, EARL'S
BARTON, BRITAIN, EARLY 11TH CENTURY**

**BAROQUE OEIL-DE-BOEUF ("OX-EYE") WINDOW,
HOTEL DES INVALIDES, PARIS, FRANCE, 1670-1708**

**SQUARE-PANELLED METAL WINDOWS, BAUHAUS
BUILDING, DESSAU, GERMANY, 1926**

The 19th century

BUILDINGS OF THE 19TH CENTURY are characterized by the use of new materials and by a great diversity of architectural styles. From the end of the 18th century, iron and steel became widely used as alternatives to wood for the framework of buildings, as in the flax-spinning mill shown here. Built in Britain in 1796, this mill exemplifies an architectural style that became common throughout the industrialized world for more than a century. The Industrial Revolution also brought mass-production of building parts – a development that enabled the British architect Sir Joseph Paxton to erect London's Crystal Palace (a building made entirely of iron and glass) in only nine months, ready for the Great Exhibition of 1851. The 19th century saw a widespread revival of older architectural styles. For example, in the USA and Germany, Neo-Greek architecture was fashionable; in Britain and France, Neo-Baroque, Neo-Byzantine, and Neo-Gothic styles (as seen in the Palace of Westminster and Tower Bridge) were dominant.

FLAX-SPINNING MILL, SHREWSBURY, BRITAIN, 1796 (BY C. BAGE)

Cast-iron wall-plate · Pitched roof · Ridge · Verge · Gutter
Machinery space
Cast-iron mortise-and-tenon joint
Inverted T-section cast-iron beam
Segmentally arched brick vault
Anchor-joint
Drain-pipe
End flange
Concrete floor
Tapering part of column
Paved ground floor
Strengthened central column

Multi-gabled roof (ridge and furrow roof) · Ridge · Furrow · Verge
Cast-iron wall-plate
Timber rafter
Gable
Gutter
Tapering part of column
Drain-pipe
Three courses of stretchers
Segmentally arched brick vault
Course of headers
Cast-iron mortise-and-tenon joint
Course of decorative headers
Tie-rod
Cast-iron cruciform column
Cast-iron lattice window
Inverted T-section cast-iron beam
Cast-iron tenon
Anchor-joint
Strengthened central column
Bonded brick wall

Stone foundation · Quoin · Jamb · Gauged arch (segmental arch of tapered bricks)

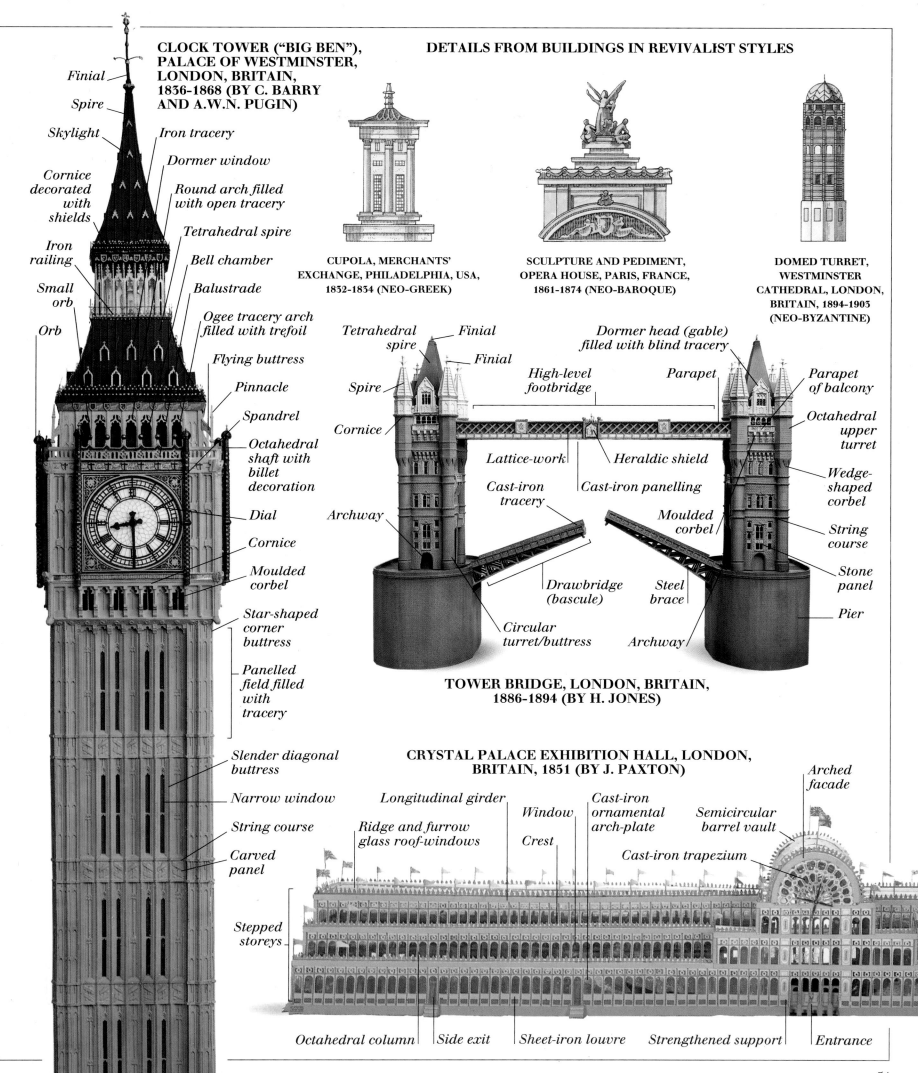

CLOCK TOWER ("BIG BEN"), PALACE OF WESTMINSTER, LONDON, BRITAIN, 1836-1868 (BY C. BARRY AND A.W.N. PUGIN)

Finial

Spire

Skylight

Cornice decorated with shields

Iron railing

Small orb

Orb

Iron tracery

Dormer window

Round arch filled with open tracery

Tetrahedral spire

Bell chamber

Balustrade

Ogee tracery arch filled with trefoil

Flying buttress

Pinnacle

Spandrel

Octahedral shaft with billet decoration

Dial

Cornice

Moulded corbel

Star-shaped corner buttress

Panelled field filled with tracery

Slender diagonal buttress

Narrow window

String course

Carved panel

DETAILS FROM BUILDINGS IN REVIVALIST STYLES

CUPOLA, MERCHANTS' EXCHANGE, PHILADELPHIA, USA, 1832-1834 (NEO-GREEK)

SCULPTURE AND PEDIMENT, OPERA HOUSE, PARIS, FRANCE, 1861-1874 (NEO-BAROQUE)

DOMED TURRET, WESTMINSTER CATHEDRAL, LONDON, BRITAIN, 1894-1903 (NEO-BYZANTINE)

Tetrahedral spire

Finial

Finial

Spire

Cornice

Archway

Cast-iron tracery

High-level footbridge

Parapet

Dormer head (gable) filled with blind tracery

Lattice-work

Heraldic shield

Cast-iron panelling

Drawbridge (bascule)

Steel brace

Circular turret/buttress

Archway

Parapet of balcony

Octahedral upper turret

Wedge-shaped corbel

String course

Moulded corbel

Stone panel

Pier

TOWER BRIDGE, LONDON, BRITAIN, 1886-1894 (BY H. JONES)

CRYSTAL PALACE EXHIBITION HALL, LONDON, BRITAIN, 1851 (BY J. PAXTON)

Longitudinal girder

Window

Ridge and furrow glass roof-windows

Crest

Cast-iron ornamental arch-plate

Arched facade

Semicircular barrel vault

Cast-iron trapezium

Stepped storeys

Octahedral column

Side exit

Sheet-iron louvre

Strengthened support

Entrance

The early 20th century

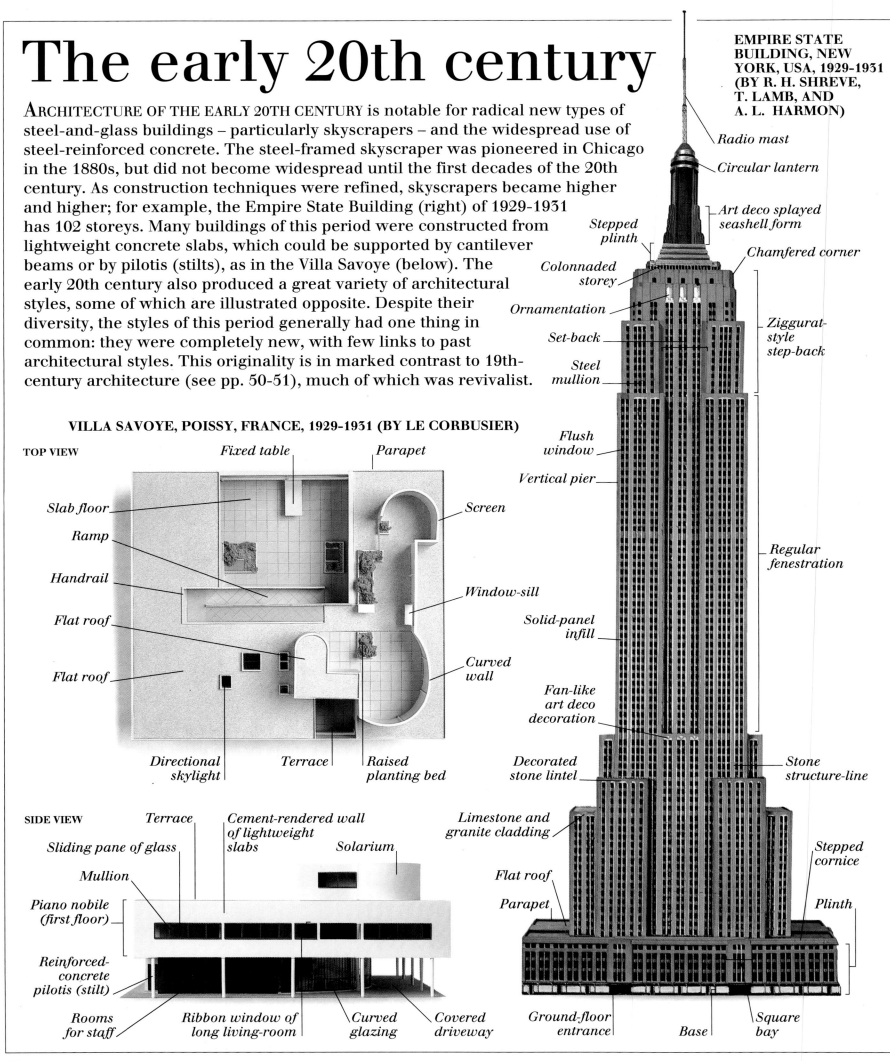

ARCHITECTURE OF THE EARLY 20TH CENTURY is notable for radical new types of steel-and-glass buildings – particularly skyscrapers – and the widespread use of steel-reinforced concrete. The steel-framed skyscraper was pioneered in Chicago in the 1880s, but did not become widespread until the first decades of the 20th century. As construction techniques were refined, skyscrapers became higher and higher; for example, the Empire State Building (right) of 1929-1931 has 102 storeys. Many buildings of this period were constructed from lightweight concrete slabs, which could be supported by cantilever beams or by pilotis (stilts), as in the Villa Savoye (below). The early 20th century also produced a great variety of architectural styles, some of which are illustrated opposite. Despite their diversity, the styles of this period generally had one thing in common: they were completely new, with few links to past architectural styles. This originality is in marked contrast to 19th-century architecture (see pp. 50-51), much of which was revivalist.

EMPIRE STATE BUILDING, NEW YORK, USA, 1929-1931 (BY R. H. SHREVE, T. LAMB, AND A. L. HARMON)

Radio mast

Circular lantern

Art deco splayed seashell form

Stepped plinth

Chamfered corner

Colonnaded storey

Ornamentation

Ziggurat-style step-back

Set-back

Steel mullion

Flush window

Vertical pier

Regular fenestration

Solid-panel infill

Fan-like art deco decoration

Decorated stone lintel

Stone structure-line

Limestone and granite cladding

Flat roof

Parapet

Stepped cornice

Plinth

Ground-floor entrance

Base

Square bay

VILLA SAVOYE, POISSY, FRANCE, 1929-1931 (BY LE CORBUSIER)

TOP VIEW

Fixed table

Parapet

Slab floor

Screen

Ramp

Handrail

Flat roof

Window-sill

Flat roof

Curved wall

Directional skylight

Terrace

Raised planting bed

SIDE VIEW

Terrace

Cement-rendered wall of lightweight slabs

Solarium

Sliding pane of glass

Mullion

Piano nobile (first floor)

Reinforced-concrete pilotis (stilt)

Rooms for staff

Ribbon window of long living-room

Curved glazing

Covered driveway

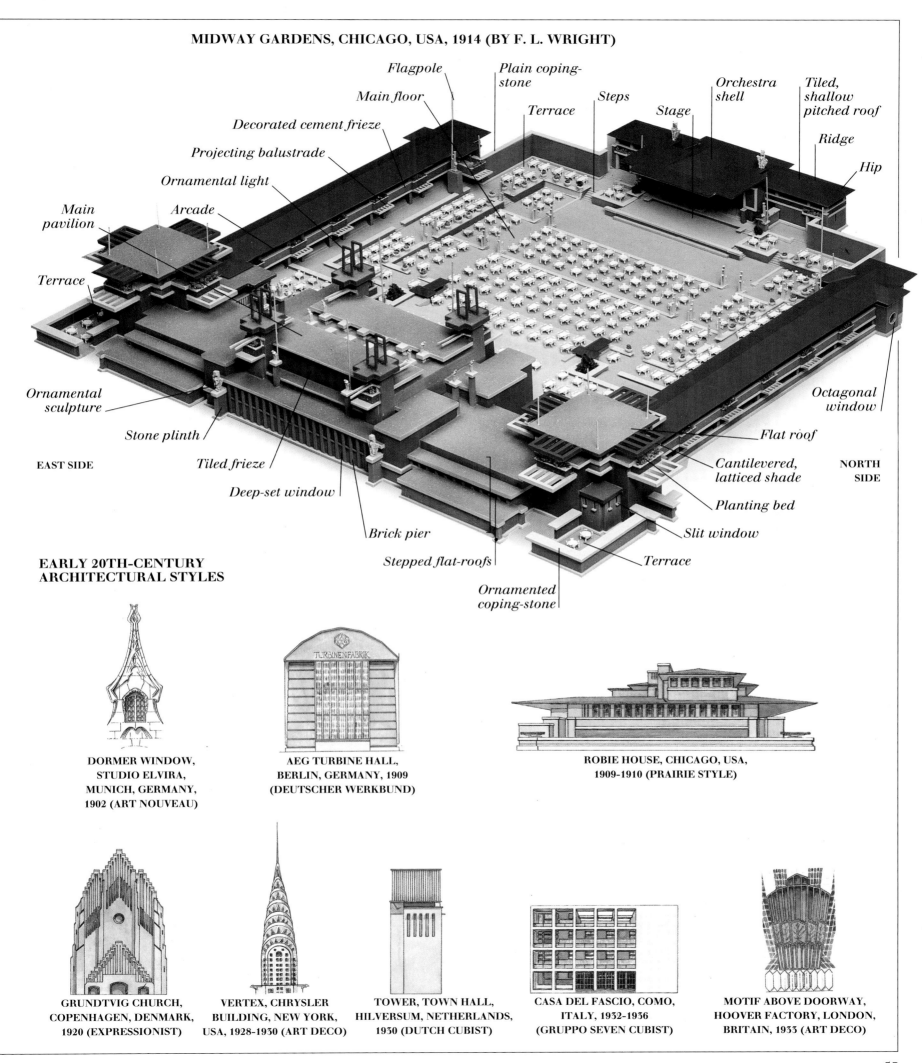

MIDWAY GARDENS, CHICAGO, USA, 1914 (BY F. L. WRIGHT)

Flagpole

Plain coping-stone

Main floor

Terrace

Steps

Stage

Orchestra shell

Tiled, shallow pitched roof

Decorated cement frieze

Ridge

Projecting balustrade

Hip

Ornamental light

Main pavilion

Arcade

Terrace

Ornamental sculpture

Stone plinth

Octagonal window

Tiled frieze

Flat roof

EAST SIDE

NORTH SIDE

Deep-set window

Cantilevered, latticed shade

Brick pier

Planting bed

Stepped flat-roofs

Slit window

Terrace

Ornamented coping-stone

EARLY 20TH-CENTURY ARCHITECTURAL STYLES

DORMER WINDOW,
STUDIO ELVIRA,
MUNICH, GERMANY,
1902 (ART NOUVEAU)

AEG TURBINE HALL,
BERLIN, GERMANY, 1909
(DEUTSCHER WERKBUND)

ROBIE HOUSE, CHICAGO, USA,
1909-1910 (PRAIRIE STYLE)

GRUNDTVIG CHURCH,
COPENHAGEN, DENMARK,
1920 (EXPRESSIONIST)

VERTEX, CHRYSLER
BUILDING, NEW YORK,
USA, 1928-1930 (ART DECO)

TOWER, TOWN HALL,
HILVERSUM, NETHERLANDS,
1930 (DUTCH CUBIST)

CASA DEL FASCIO, COMO,
ITALY, 1932-1936
(GRUPPO SEVEN CUBIST)

MOTIF ABOVE DOORWAY,
HOOVER FACTORY, LONDON,
BRITAIN, 1933 (ART DECO)

Modern buildings 1

ARCHITECTURE SINCE ABOUT THE 1950s is generally known as modern architecture. One of its main influences has been functionalism – a belief that a building's function should be apparent in its design. Both the Centre Georges Pompidou (below and opposite) and the Hong Kong and Shanghai Bank (see pp. 56-57) are functionalist buildings: on each, elements of engineering and the building's services are clearly visible on the outside. In the 1980s, some architects rejected functionalism in favour of post-modernism, in which historical styles – particularly neoclassicism – were revived, using modern building materials and techniques. In many modern buildings, walls are made of glass or concrete hung from a frame, as in the Kawana House (right); this type of wall construction is known as curtain walling. Other modern construction techniques include the intricate interlocking of concrete vaults – as in the Sydney Opera House (see pp. 56-57) – and the use of high-tension beams to create complex roof shapes, such as the paraboloid roof of the Church of St. Pierre de Libreville (see pp. 56-57).

Solar panel

Concrete frame

Pile foundation

Raft   *Composite cladding-panel*

SIDE VIEW

Rocker-beam

Curtain walling

Lattice-beam

Floor-beam connection   *Floor*

FRONT VIEW

SERVICES FACADE, CENTRE GEORGES POMPIDOU, PARIS, FRANCE, 1977 (BY R. PIANO AND R. ROGERS)

Water-pipe

Metal-faced, fire-resistant panel

Air-conditioning duct

Cooling tower

Grand gallery level

Main gallery levels

Library level

Administrative level

Mezzanine gallery level

Reception level

Staircase to grand hall

Electrical plant

Water-cooled, fire-resistant column

Continuous glazing

Tinted glass

Services entrance

PRINCIPAL FACADE, CENTRE GEORGES POMPIDOU

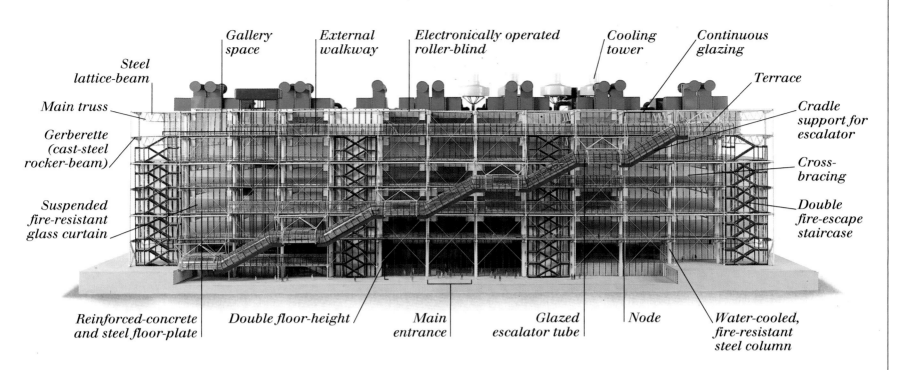

Steel lattice-beam

Main truss

Gerberette (cast-steel rocker-beam)

Suspended fire-resistant glass curtain

Gallery space

External walkway

Electronically operated roller-blind

Cooling tower

Continuous glazing

Terrace

Cradle support for escalator

Cross-bracing

Double fire-escape staircase

Reinforced-concrete and steel floor-plate

Double floor-height

Main entrance

Glazed escalator tube

Node

Water-cooled, fire-resistant steel column

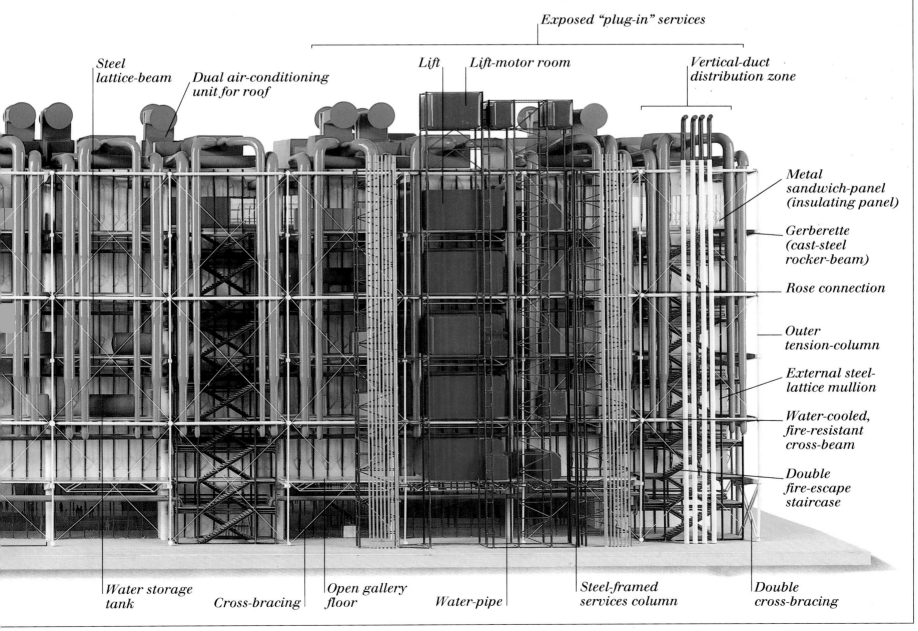

Exposed "plug-in" services

Steel lattice-beam

Dual air-conditioning unit for roof

Lift

Lift-motor room

Vertical-duct distribution zone

Metal sandwich-panel (insulating panel)

Gerberette (cast-steel rocker-beam)

Rose connection

Outer tension-column

External steel-lattice mullion

Water-cooled, fire-resistant cross-beam

Double fire-escape staircase

Water storage tank

Cross-bracing

Open gallery floor

Water-pipe

Steel-framed services column

Double cross-bracing

Modern buildings 2

HONG KONG AND SHANGHAI BANK, HONG KONG, 1981-1985 (BY N. FOSTER)

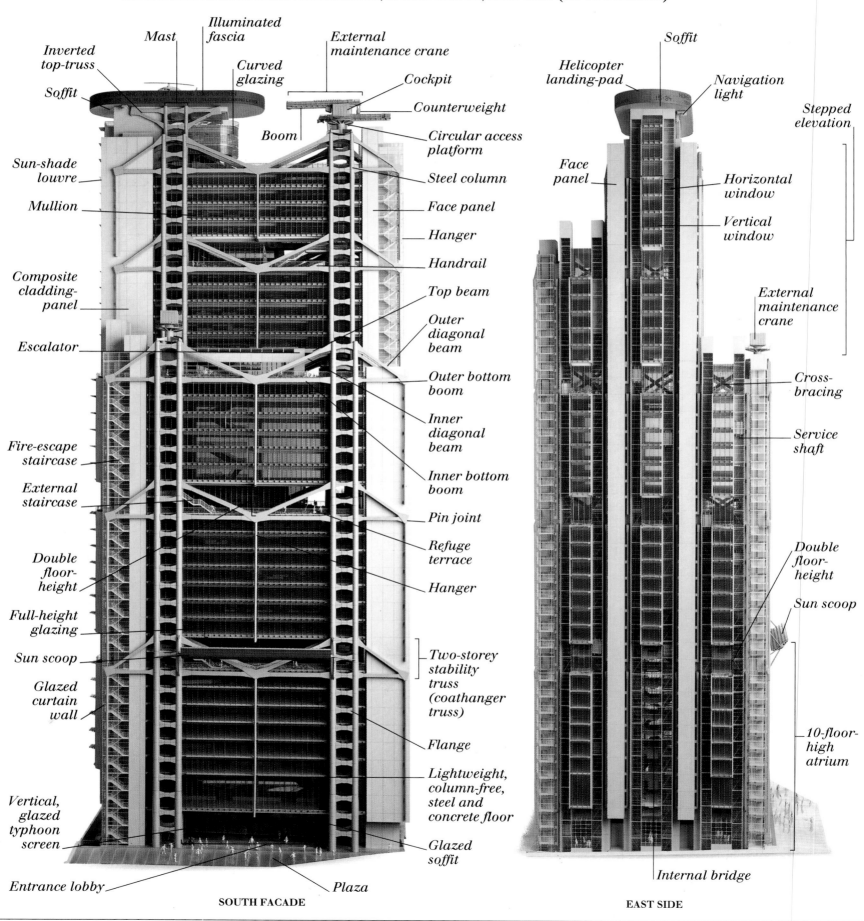

Inverted top-truss

Mast

Illuminated fascia

External maintenance crane

Soffit

Helicopter landing-pad

Soffit

Navigation light

Stepped elevation

Curved glazing

Cockpit

Counterweight

Boom

Circular access platform

Face panel

Soffit

Sun-shade louvre

Steel column

Horizontal window

Mullion

Face panel

Vertical window

Hanger

Handrail

Composite cladding-panel

Top beam

Outer diagonal beam

External maintenance crane

Escalator

Outer bottom boom

Cross-bracing

Inner diagonal beam

Service shaft

Fire-escape staircase

Inner bottom boom

External staircase

Pin joint

Double floor-height

Refuge terrace

Double floor-height

Hanger

Full-height glazing

Sun scoop

Sun scoop

Two-storey stability truss (coathanger truss)

Glazed curtain wall

10-floor-high atrium

Vertical, glazed typhoon screen

Flange

Lightweight, column-free, steel and concrete floor

Glazed soffit

Entrance lobby

Plaza

Internal bridge

SOUTH FACADE

EAST SIDE

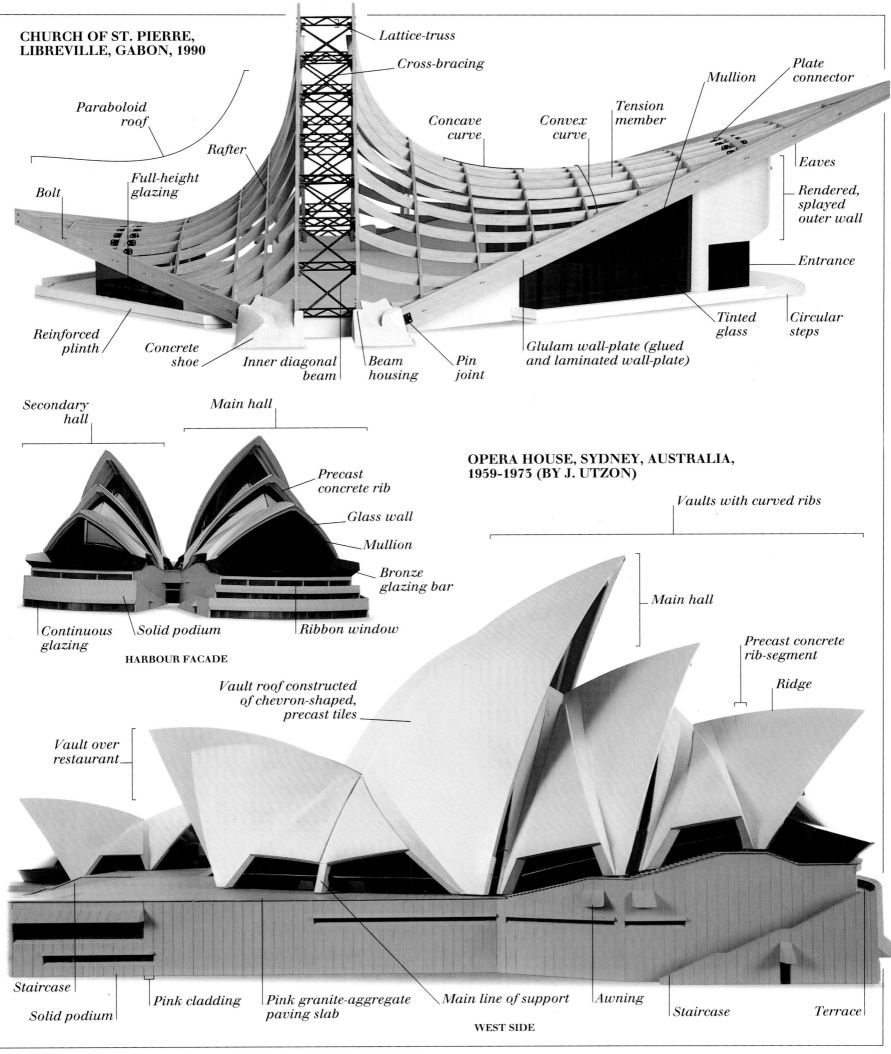

CHURCH OF ST. PIERRE, LIBREVILLE, GABON, 1990

Lattice-truss

Cross-bracing

Paraboloid roof

Mullion

Plate connector

Concave curve

Convex curve

Tension member

Rafter

Full-height glazing

Bolt

Eaves

Rendered, splayed outer wall

Reinforced plinth

Concrete shoe

Inner diagonal beam

Beam housing

Pin joint

Entrance

Tinted glass

Circular steps

Glulam wall-plate (glued and laminated wall-plate)

Secondary hall

Main hall

OPERA HOUSE, SYDNEY, AUSTRALIA, 1959-1973 (BY J. UTZON)

Precast concrete rib

Glass wall

Mullion

Bronze glazing bar

Continuous glazing

Solid podium

Ribbon window

HARBOUR FACADE

Vaults with curved ribs

Main hall

Precast concrete rib-segment

Ridge

Vault roof constructed of chevron-shaped, precast tiles

Vault over restaurant

Staircase

Solid podium

Pink cladding

Pink granite-aggregate paving slab

Main line of support

Awning

Staircase

Terrace

WEST SIDE

57

Architectural styles

BUILDINGS CAN BE CLASSIFIED according to which of the various architectural styles they exemplify. There are three main criteria used to define a building's style: design, proportions, and ornamentation. These criteria may be influenced by various factors, including the function of a building, the materials and building techniques available, and the interests of a building's patron. The chart below shows the major architectural styles throughout the ages and across the world, with illustrations of important buildings of each style. From the chart it is possible to identify certain recurring trends, such as the importance of continuity in Far Eastern and Indian buildings, the innovative character of European architecture since medieval times, the enduring use of classical motifs, and the worldwide influence of Islamic themes.

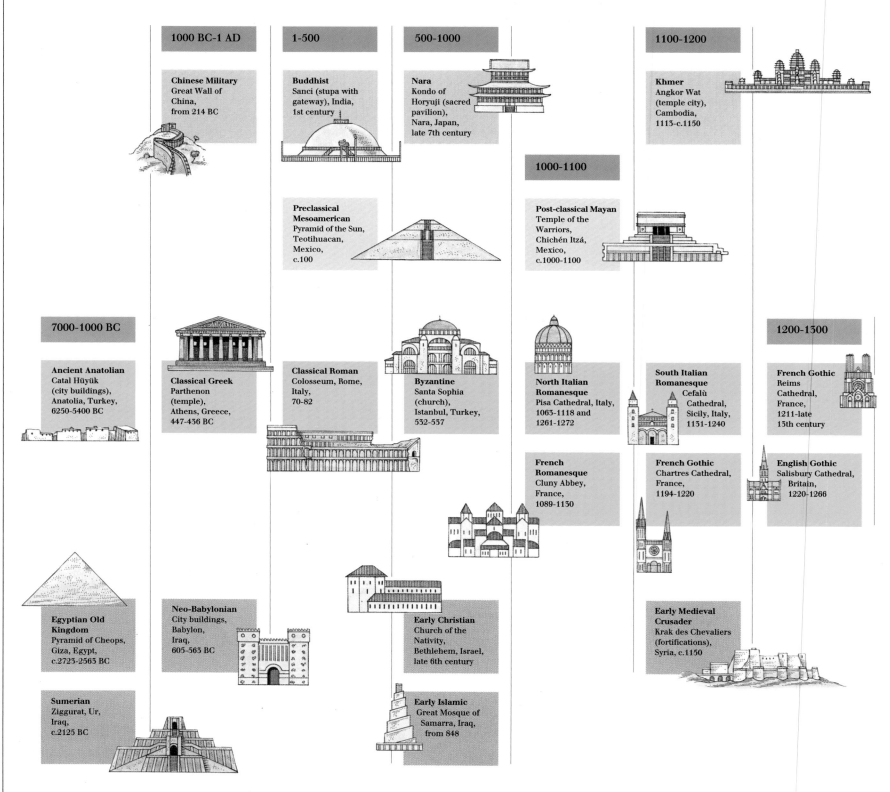

1000 BC-1 AD

Chinese Military
Great Wall of China, from 214 BC

1-500

Buddhist
Sanci (stupa with gateway), India, 1st century

500-1000

Nara
Kondo of Horyuji (sacred pavilion), Nara, Japan, late 7th century

1100-1200

Khmer
Angkor Wat (temple city), Cambodia, 1113-c.1150

1000-1100

Preclassical Mesoamerican
Pyramid of the Sun, Teotihuacan, Mexico, c.100

Post-classical Mayan
Temple of the Warriors, Chichén Itzá, Mexico, c.1000-1100

7000-1000 BC

Ancient Anatolian
Catal Hüyük (city buildings), Anatolia, Turkey, 6250-5400 BC

Classical Greek
Parthenon (temple), Athens, Greece, 447-436 BC

Classical Roman
Colosseum, Rome, Italy, 70-82

Byzantine
Santa Sophia (church), Istanbul, Turkey, 532-537

North Italian Romanesque
Pisa Cathedral, Italy, 1063-1118 and 1261-1272

South Italian Romanesque
Cefalù Cathedral, Sicily, Italy, 1131-1240

1200-1300

French Gothic
Reims Cathedral, France, 1211-late 13th century

French Romanesque
Cluny Abbey, France, 1089-1130

French Gothic
Chartres Cathedral, France, 1194-1220

English Gothic
Salisbury Cathedral, Britain, 1220-1266

Egyptian Old Kingdom
Pyramid of Cheops, Giza, Egypt, c.2725-2563 BC

Neo-Babylonian
City buildings, Babylon, Iraq, 605-563 BC

Early Christian
Church of the Nativity, Bethlehem, Israel, late 6th century

Early Medieval Crusader
Krak des Chevaliers (fortifications), Syria, c.1150

Sumerian
Ziggurat, Ur, Iraq, c.2125 BC

Early Islamic
Great Mosque of Samarra, Iraq, from 848

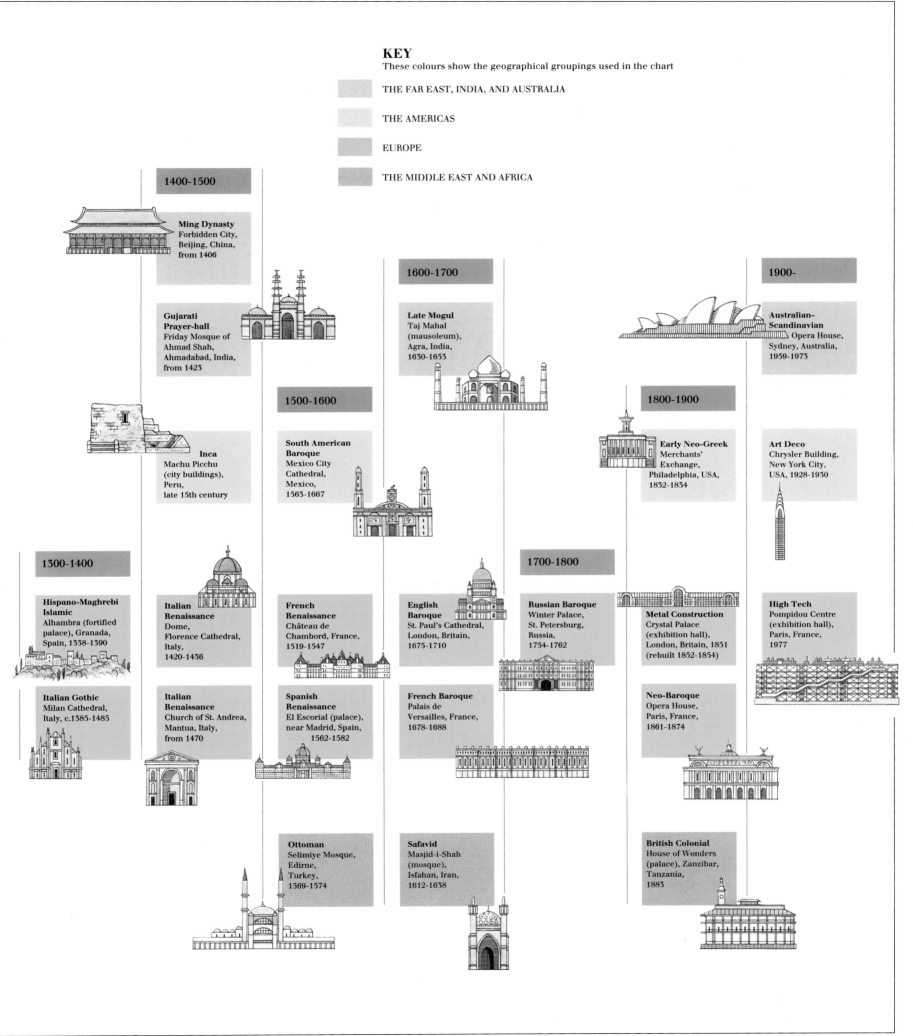

KEY

These colours show the geographical groupings used in the chart

THE FAR EAST, INDIA, AND AUSTRALIA

THE AMERICAS

EUROPE

THE MIDDLE EAST AND AFRICA

1400-1500

Ming Dynasty
Forbidden City,
Beijing, China,
from 1406

Gujarati Prayer-hall
Friday Mosque of
Ahmad Shah,
Ahmadabad, India,
from 1423

Inca
Machu Picchu
(city buildings),
Peru,
late 15th century

1600-1700

Late Mogul
Taj Mahal
(mausoleum),
Agra, India,
1630-1653

1900-

Australian-Scandinavian
Opera House,
Sydney, Australia,
1959-1973

1500-1600

South American Baroque
Mexico City
Cathedral,
Mexico,
1563-1667

1800-1900

Early Neo-Greek
Merchants'
Exchange,
Philadelphia, USA,
1832-1834

Art Deco
Chrysler Building,
New York City,
USA, 1928-1930

1300-1400

Hispano-Maghrebi Islamic
Alhambra (fortified
palace), Granada,
Spain, 1338-1390

Italian Renaissance
Dome,
Florence Cathedral,
Italy,
1420-1436

French Renaissance
Château de
Chambord, France,
1519-1547

English Baroque
St. Paul's Cathedral,
London, Britain,
1675-1710

Russian Baroque
Winter Palace,
St. Petersburg,
Russia,
1754-1762

1700-1800

Metal Construction
Crystal Palace
(exhibition hall),
London, Britain, 1851
(rebuilt 1852-1854)

High Tech
Pompidou Centre
(exhibition hall),
Paris, France,
1977

Italian Gothic
Milan Cathedral,
Italy, c.1385-1485

Italian Renaissance
Church of St. Andrea,
Mantua, Italy,
from 1470

Spanish Renaissance
El Escorial (palace),
near Madrid, Spain,
1562-1582

French Baroque
Palais de
Versailles, France,
1678-1688

Neo-Baroque
Opera House,
Paris, France,
1861-1874

Ottoman
Selimiye Mosque,
Edirne,
Turkey,
1569-1574

Safavid
Masjid-i-Shah
(mosque),
Isfahan, Iran,
1612-1638

British Colonial
House of Wonders
(palace), Zanzibar,
Tanzania,
1883

Index

A

Abacus
  Ancient Egyptian temple 7
  Ancient Greek building 8
  Medieval church 21
  Neoclassical building 35
Abbey of St. Foi, Conques,
    France 20
Abutment 38-39
Abutment pier 15
Acanthus leaf 8, 36
Acropolis, Athens, Greece 8
Acroterion 8-9
Aedicule
  Ancient Roman
    building 11
  Renaissance building
    26, 28
AEG Turbine Hall, Berlin,
    Germany 53
Air-conditioning 54-55
Air duct 15
Aisle
  Ancient Egyptian temple 6
  Cathedral dome 38
  Gothic church 22, 24-25
  Medieval church 20-21
Alhambra, Granada, Spain
    42, 59
Altar 22
Ambulatory corridor 13
Amphitheatre 12-13
Anchor-joint 50
Ancient Anatolian style 58
Ancient Egyptian
    buildings 6-7
Ancient Greek buildings
    8-9, 10
Ancient Roman buildings
    10-13, 26
  Tile 17
  Window 48
Angkor Wat, Cambodia 58
Angle buttress 23, 24
Anglo-Saxon style 47, 49
Angoulême Cathedral,
    France 20-21
Angular cincture 16
Annulet 8
Anta 9
Antarala 44-45
Antefixa 9
Apse 13, 21, 33
Arabesque
  Ceiling panel 36-37
  Neoclassical moulding 32
  Islamic building 42-43
Arcade
  Ancient Roman
    building 12-13
  Baroque church 31-33
  Gothic building 22-23
  Medieval church 20-21
  Twentieth-century
    building 53
Arched brace 25
Arched doorway 26, 27, 47
Arched facade 51
Arches 14, 38-39
  Ancient Roman building
    10, 12-13
  Asian building 44-45
  Baroque church 31, 32
  Cathedral dome 41
  Cathedral pier 15
  Door 46
  French temple 38-39
  Gothic church 22-25
  Islamic building 42-43
  Medieval building 18-21
  Nineteenth-century
    building 50-51
  Renaissance building
    26-27
Architectural styles 58-59
Architrave
  Ancient Egyptian
    temple 6-7
  Ancient Greek temple 9
  Ancient Roman building
    11, 13
  Baroque church 31-33
  French temple 39

Gothic building 25
Neoclassical building
    30, 34-35
Renaissance building
    28-29
Archivolt
  Baroque church 31, 33
  French temple 39
  Gothic church 23
  Medieval building 19-20
  Renaissance building 29
Arch of Titus, Italy 11
Arch-plate 51
Archway 51
Arris 14
  Medieval church 21
  Moulding 39
Art deco style 53, 59
  Doorway 47
  Twentieth-century
    building 52, 53
Art nouveau style 53
  Doorway 47
Ashlar 12, 16, 40
Asian buildings 44-45
Asphalt 16
Astragal 40
Atlas 34
Atrium 56
Attached column
  Ancient Roman
    building 13
  Baroque church 32
  Gothic building 25
  Medieval building 20-21
  Neoclassical building 31
Attic
  Baroque church 32-33
  Cathedral dome 41
  Neoclassical building
    30, 35
Auda 45
Auditorium 31
Aureole 23
Australian-Scandinavian
    style 59
Awning 57
Axle-pulley 49

B

Bage, C. 50
Bagneux Church, France
    20-21
Bailey 18
Balcony 51
  Islamic tomb 43
  Nineteenth-century
    building 51
  Renaissance theatre 29
  Rococo style 30, 34
Ballflowers 22-23
Baluster
  Asian building 44
  Gothic building 25
  Neoclassical building 35
Balustrade
  Asian building 44
  Baroque church 31-32
  Cathedral dome 41
  Gothic church 24-25
  Neoclassical building
    30, 35
  Nineteenth-century
    building 51
  Renaissance theatre 29
  Twentieth-century
    building 53
Bank of England, London,
    Britain 34
Banqueting House, Whitehall
    Palace, London, Britain
    36-37
Barge-board 14
Baroque style 30-35, 59
  Window 49
Barrel vault 38-39
  Ancient Roman building
    11-12
  Baroque church 31
  Cathedral pier 15
  Medieval church 20

Nineteenth-century
    building 51
Barry, C. 51
Bascule 51
Base
  Ancient Greek temple 9
  Ancient Roman building
    11, 13
  Asian building 45
  Baroque church 31, 33
  Cathedral pier 15
  Dome 38, 40, 41
  French temple 39
  Gothic church 22, 24
  Medieval church 21
  Neoclassical building
    30, 35
  Renaissance theatre 29
  Twentieth-century
    building 52
Basement 35
Baseplate 40
Basilican system 20
Basilica of St. Madeleine,
    Vezelay, France 20
Basket arch 24, 38
Bas-relief carving 45
Bastille, Paris, France 18
Batten 47
Battlemented building 18-19
Battlemented cornice 23
Battlements 18
Bauhaus Building, Dessau,
    Germany 48-49
Bauhaus window 49
Bay 20, 21, 52
Bay-leaf garland 32
Bay window 29
Bead 46
Bead moulding 7
Beam
  Crown-post 16
  Gothic church 25
  High-tension 54
  Modern building 55-57
  Nineteenth-century
    building 50
Becket Chapel, London,
    Britain 19
Bed-joint 14
Belfry 33
Bell chamber 51
Bell-shaped dome 45
Belvedere 28
Bevelled panel 47
Beverley Minster, Yorkshire,
    Britain 38
"Big Ben", Palace of
    Westminster, London,
    Britain 51
Binder 12, 14
Blind arch
  Asian building 45
  Cathedral dome 41
  Gothic church 22
Blind door 30
Blind tracery 51
Blind trefoil 25
Blind window 30
Block carving 22
Board-and-plaster ceiling 36
Boarding 12
Bolection moulding 46-47
Bolt 48, 57
Bonded brick wall 50
Bonding 14
  English bond 14, 39
  Flemish bond 14, 17
  Stretcher bond 14, 17
Bonnet hip-tile 17
Boom 56
Border 48
Boss 20-21
Bow front 35
Bowtell moulding 27
Box 29
Box sash-window 49
Brace 14, 39
  Asian building 44
  Crown-post roof 16
  Dome 40
  Door 46-47
  Gothic building 25
  King-post roof 16
  Neoclassical building 31

Nineteenth-century
    building 51
  Queen-post roof 16
  Timber-framed house 14
Bracket
  Baroque church 31
  Cathedral dome 38
  Cathedral pier 15
  Ceiling panel 36
  Gothic building 25
  Islamic tomb 43
  Medieval building 18
  Neoclassical building 30
  Renaissance building 27
  Timber-framed house 14
  Victorian chimney 17
Breakfast-room 35
Breastsummer 14
Bressumer 14
Bricklaying 14
Brick pier 53
Brick vault 50
Brick wall 14, 50
Bridges
  London Bridge 18-19
  Medieval castle 19
  Modern building 56
British colonial style 59
Broken pediment 33
Buddhist style 44, 58
Burmese pagoda 44
Butt-hinge 47
Buttress 38
  Baroque church 30-33
  Cathedral pier 15
  Dome 40
  Gothic church 22-25
  Medieval building 18,
    20-21
  Nineteenth-century
    building 51
Byzantine style 49, 58

C

Caernarvon Castle,
    Britain 18
Came 48
Campaniform capital 6
Campanile 29
Candelabrum 28
Canopy 24
Cantilever beams 52
Cantilevered shade 53
Capital
  Ancient Egyptian
    building 6-7
  Ancient Greek
    building 6, 8-9
  Ancient Roman
    building 6, 11, 13
  Asian building 44, 45
  Baroque church 31, 33
  Cathedral dome 41
  Cathedral pier 15
  Domed roof 40
  French temple 39
  Islamic mosque 42
  Medieval building 19-21
  Neoclassical building
    30, 35
  Ptolemaic-Roman period 7
  Renaissance building
    28-29
  Romanesque style 20
Cartouche 6
Carved stone 42
Carving 14
  Asian building 44-45
  Gothic building 22
Casa de las Conchas,
    Salamanca, Spain 28
Casa del Fascio, Como, Italy
    53
Casement-window 48
Cast-iron 50-51
Castles, medieval 18-19
Cast-steel 55
Catal Hüyük, Anatolia,
    Turkey 58
Cathedral of St. Lazare,
    Autun, France 20

Cauliculus 8
Cavetto moulding
  Ancient Egyptian
    building 6-7
  Baroque church 31
  French temple 39
  Gothic building 24
  Renaissance building 29
  Timber-framed house 14
Cavity wall 14
Cefalù Cathedral, Sicily,
    Italy 58
Ceilings 36-37, 38
  Ancient Roman
    building 11
  Panels 36-37
Cell 21, 39
Cella 9, 11, 39
Cement-rendered wall 52
Censer 42
Centre Georges Pompidou,
    Paris, France 54-55
Chain motif 45
Chajya 43
Chamber 13, 45
Chamfered corner 39, 42, 52
Channel 8
Chapel
  Baroque church 31
  Gothic church 22
  Medieval church 21
Chapel pier 19
Chapter-house 24
Chartres Cathedral,
    France 58
Chataya arch 45
Chattaya 44-45
Chattra 45
Chattravali 45
Château de Blois, France 28
Château de Chambord,
    France 28, 59
Château de Montal, Lot,
    France 26, 28-29
Chattravali 45
Chemise 18-19
Cherub 24, 36-37
Chevet 21
Chichén Itzá, Mexico 58
Chimneys 16-17
Chimney-shaft 19
Chimney-stack 17, 28, 35
Chinese military style 58
Choir
  Gothic church 22, 24
  Medieval church 20-21
Choir-aisle 22
Choir-screen 22
Choir-stall 22
Christian architecture 20
Chrysler Building, New York,
    USA 47, 53, 59
Church of St. Andrea,
    Mantua, Italy 59
Church of St. Botolph,
    Norfolk, Britain 25
Church of St. Eustache,
    Paris, France 29
Church of St. George in the
    East, London, Britain
    30, 33
Church of St. Maclou, Rouen,
    France 22, 24
Church of St. Maria della
    Salute, Venice, Italy 30
Church of St. Maria della
    Vittoria, Rome, Italy 30
Church of St. Paul-St. Louis,
    Paris, France 30-31
Church of St. Pierre de
    Libreville, Gabon 54, 57
Church of St. Serge, Angers,
    France 21
Church of St. Zaccaria,
    Venice, Italy 47
Church of Santa Sophia,
    Turkey 41, 58
Church of the Nativity,
    Bethlehem, Israel 58
Church of the Sorbonne,
    Paris, France 30
Church-roof boss 20
Cincture 16, 29
Cinquefoil moulding 23
Circle 31
Cirque Napoleon, Paris,
    France 30-31

Cladding
  Modern building 54, 56-57
  Tiled roof 14, 17
  Twentieth-century
    building 52
Cladding-panel 54
Classical Greek style 58
Classical Roman style 58
Classical-style architecture
    26, 30, 34
Clay daub 13, 14
Clay tile 16-17
Clerestory
  Ancient Egyptian temple 7
  Baroque church 31
  Cathedral pier 15
  Gothic church 24
Clock tower 51
Cloister 24
Closer 14
Cluny Abbey, France 58
Clustered column 21
Coat of arms 48
Cockspur-pattern
    handle 48
Coffer 11, 39
Coffered arch 15
Coffered vault 39
Coffering 27
Collar 25
Collar-beam 14, 16, 25
Collar purlin 14, 16
Cologne Cathedral, Germany
    46-47
Colonette
  Gothic church 25
  Islamic building 42
  Medieval building 19-21
  Neoclassical building 31
  Renaissance building 26
Colonnade
  Ancient Greek
    building 8-9
  Ancient Roman
    building 10-11
  Cathedral dome 38, 41
  Neoclassical building 35
Colonnaded storey 52
Colosseum, Rome, Italy
    10, 12-13, 58
Column 14
  Ancient Egyptian
    building 6-7
  Ancient Greek
    building 6, 8
  Ancient Roman building
    6, 10-11, 13
  Baroque church 32-33
  Cathedral dome 41
  French temple 39
  Gothic church 25
  Islamic mosque 42
  Medieval church 20-21
  Modern building 54-56
  Neoclassical building
    30-31, 35
  Nineteenth-century
    building 50-51
  Renaissance building 29
Common rafter
  Crown-post roof 16
  Dome 40
  Gothic building 25
  Tiled roof 17
  Timber-framed house 14
Compass 39
Composite capital 15, 30
Composite column 30
Composite pilaster 15, 30
Compound pier 20-21
Concave brace 14, 29
Concave moulding 34
Concave wall 30, 33
Concrete 52, 55
Concrete floor 50, 56
Concrete frame 54
Concrete rib 57
Concrete shoe 57
Concrete wall 11, 13, 54
Conical dome 28
Conical spire 18, 28
Contant d'Ivry, P. 30
Convex portico 35
Cooling tower 54-55
Coping-stone 53

60

Copper tingle 17
Corbel
　Cathedral dome 41
　Medieval building 19, 21
　Neoclassical building 34
　Nineteenth-century
　　building 51
　Renaissance building 29
　Rococo style 30
Corinthian capital 8
　Ancient Roman
　　building 11
　Baroque church 31, 33
　Cathedral pier 15
Corinthian column 11,
　31-32
Corinthian entablature 11
Corinthian half-column 12
Corinthian order 8, 10
Corinthian pilaster
　Ancient Roman
　　building 11-12
　Baroque church 32-33
Corner post 14
Cornice
　Ancient Egyptian
　　temple 6-7
　Ancient Greek
　　building 8-9
　Ancient Roman
　　building 10-13
　Asian building 45
　Baroque church 31-33
　Cathedral pier 15
　Dome 38, 40
　French temple 39
　Gothic church 22-25
　Islamic tomb 43
　Medieval building
　　18-19, 21
　Neoclassical building
　　30-31, 34-35
　Nineteenth-century
　　building 51
　Renaissance building
　　26-29
　Twentieth-century
　　building 52
Cornucopia 32, 37
Corona 27
Corridor 13, 15
Coucy-le-Château, Aisne,
　France 18-19
Counterweight 56
Couronnement 24
Course
　Asian building 45
　Brick 14
　Medieval building 18-19
　Neoclassical building 35
　Nineteenth-century
　　building 50-51
　Victorian chimney 17
Courtyard 13, 18
Coussinet 8
Coved dome 30, 39
Crane 56
Crenel 18
Crenellations 18
Crepidoma 9, 33
Crest 31, 42, 51
Crocket 23-24
Cronaca 26
Cross
　Baroque church 32
　Dome 40-41
　Motif 41
Cross-bracing 55-57
Crossing 21-22, 29
Crossing tower 20
Crown 17, 38, 44
Crowning cornice
　Ancient Roman
　　building 12, 13
　Baroque church 31
　Renaissance building
　　26-27
Crown-post 14, 16
Crown-post roof 16
Cruciform column 50
Cruciform pedestal 33, 41
Cruck frame 18
Crypt 15, 19
Crypt-window 33
Crystal Palace Exhibition
　Hall, London, Britain
　50-51, 59
Cuneus 13
Cupola
　Baroque church 31
　Medieval building 18
　Nineteenth-century
　　building 51

Curtain 29, 55
Curtain wall 18, 54, 56
Curved buttress 30-33
Curved cornice 10
Curvilinear tracery 22, 24
Cushion 8
Cusp
　Asian building 42
　Gothic building 24-25
　Timber-framed
　　house 14
Cusped arch 43
Cyma recta 27
Cyma reversa 8, 24
Cymatium 27

D

Dado
　Baroque church 33
　French temple 39
　Neoclassical building 31
　Renaissance building 28
Dagger 24
Dagoba stupa 44-45
Da Maiano, B. 26
Dancette-pattern mosaic 43
Da Sangallo, G. 26
Daub 14
Dentil
　Ancient Roman
　　building 10
　Baroque church 31, 33
　Cathedral dome 41
　French temple 39
　Neoclassical building 30
　Renaissance building 27
　Tiled roof 17
Depressed arch
　Ancient Roman
　　building 10
　Islamic building 42-43
　Timber-framed house 14
Deutscher Werkbund
　style 53
Dial 51
Diaper work 48
Dog-leg staircase 33
Domed roof 43
Domed turret 51
Dome metalling 40
Dome of the Rock,
　Jerusalem, Israel 41
Domes 38, 40-41
　Ancient Roman
　　building 10
　Asian building 44-45
　Baroque church 32-33
　Cathedral pier 15
　French temple 39
　Islamic building 42
　Medieval building 19, 21
　Neoclassical building 30
　Renaissance building
　　27-29, 59
Dome timbering 40
Donjon 18-19
Doorbell 47
Door jamb 30
Doorknob 47
Door-knocker 47
Door rail 46
Doors 46-47
　Ancient Egyptian
　　tomb 6-7
　Ancient Roman
　　building 11
　Baroque church 31
　Neoclassical building 30
　Renaissance theatre 29
　Timber-framed house 14
Doorway 47
　Baroque church 31, 33
　Renaissance building
　　26-27
　Twentieth-century
　　building 53
Doric capital 8
Doric column 8
Doric half-column 12
Doric order 8
Dormer head 51
Dormer window 28, 51, 53
Double-glazed unit 49
Drain-pipe 50
Dravidian finial 45
Dravidian style 44
Drawbridge 51
Drawbridge windlass 19
Dressing-room 29

Drip-cap 34
Drum 40
　Ancient Greek building 8
　Baroque church 33
　Cathedral dome 41
Dubika 44
Duct 15, 54, 55
Dutch cubist style 53

E

Early Christian building 58
Early English Perpendicular-
　style tracery 24
Early English-style window
　24
Early medieval crusader
　style 58
Early Neo-Greek style 59
Earthenware tile 42
East Asian buildings 44-45
Eating room 35
Eaves
　Ancient Greek building 9
　Ancient Roman
　　building 10, 12
　Crown-post roof 16
　Islamic tomb 43
　Modern building 57
　Neoclassical building 34
　Renaissance building 29
　Tiled roof 17
　Timber-framed house 14
Eaves board 44
Echinus 8
Edge-halfed scarf-joint 16
Egyptian building 6-7, 46
Egyptian old kingdom
　style 58
Eighteenth-century
　building 50, 59
　Baroque building 33
　Neoclassical building
　　30, 34-35
Eighth-century building
　44-45
El-Ainyi Mosque, Cairo,
　Egypt 42
El Escorial Palace, Madrid,
　Spain 59
Elevation 56
Eleventh-century building
　18, 20, 49
Ellipsoid doorway 47
Ellipsoid orb 40
Embrasure 18-19, 21
Empire State Building, New
　York, USA 52
Enamel 42, 43
Engaged column 21
Engaged pediment 10-11
Engineering 54
Engineering brick 14
English baroque style
　52-53, 59
English bond brickwork
　14, 39
English Decorated style 22
English Gothic style 58
English Perpendicular
　style 22, 24
Entablature
　Ancient Greek building 8
　Ancient Roman
　　building 10-13
　Baroque church 32-33
　Cathedral dome 41
　Cathedral pier 15
　French temple 39
　Neoclassical building
　　30-31, 34-35
Entasis 9
Entrance
　Islamic tomb 43
　Medieval building 18-19
　Modern building 54-57
　Neoclassical building 35
　Nineteenth-century
　　building 51
　Twentieth-century
　　building 52
Entresol 19
Erechtheion, Athens,
　Greece 47
Escalator 55-56
Escutcheon 47
Euthynteria 8
Expressionist style 53
Extrados 38-39, 48

F

Facade
　Ancient Greek building 9
　Ancient Roman
　　building 13
　Baroque church 32-33
　Gothic church 22-24
　Modern building 54-57
　Neoclassical building
　　30, 35
　Nineteenth-century
　　building 51
　Renaissance building 26
Facade pediment 33
Facade wall 22
Face 14
False door 6-7
Fanlight 48
Fan vault 38-39
Far Eastern buildings 58-59
Fascia
　Ancient Roman
　　building 11-12
　Baroque church 31, 33
Dome 40
　Domed roof 40
　French temple 39
　Gothic building 24
　Medieval building 19, 21
　Modern building 56
　Neoclassical building 34
　Renaissance building
　　28-29
Fenestration 26, 52
Festoon
　Ancient Roman building
　　10-11
　Cathedral dome 41
　Cathedral pier 15
　Neoclassical building
　　30-31
Fifteenth century
　Mihrab 42
　Renaissance building
　　26-27
　Style 10, 22, 59
　Terraces 44
　Timber-framed house 14
　Tracery 24
Fillet
　Ancient Greek temple 9
　Ceiling panel 37
　Dome 40
　French temple 39
　Gothic building 22
　Neoclassical moulding 32
　Renaissance building
　　27, 29
Finial
　Asian building 44-45
　Baroque church 31, 33
　Gothic church 22-23
　Islamic building 42-43
　Medieval building 20
　Neoclassical building 30
　Nineteenth-century
　　building 51
，　Renaissance building 28
　Roof 16
Fire-escape 55-56
Fireplace 16, 18-19
Fire-resistant curtain 55
Fire-resistant panel 54
First century
　Building 10-12
　Style 58
Fish-scale tile 28-29, 40
Flagpole 53
Flamboyant tracery 24
Flange 50, 56
Flat roof 16
　Ancient Egyptian
　　building 6
　Neoclassical building 35
　Twentieth-century
　　building 52-53
Flat soffit 12
Flavian amphitheatre,
　Italy 12
Flax-spinning mill,
　Shrewsbury, Britain 50
Flemish bond 14, 17
Flint facing-brick 14
Floor 36
　Cathedral pier 15
　Modern building 54-56
　Nineteenth-century
　　building 50
　Twentieth-century
　　building 52-53
Floorboard 12, 14, 40

Floor-joist 12, 14
Florence Cathedral, Italy
　27, 41, 59
Flue 16
Flush window 52
Fluted pilaster 10
Fluted pinnacle 33
Fluted shaft 30
Fluting 9, 11
Flying buttress
　Gothic building 22-25
　Medieval building 18,
　　20-21
　Nineteenth-century
　　building 51
Foliated capital 21
Foliated frieze 21, 31
Foliated panel 31
Foliated scrollwork 24
Foliated volute 28
Footbridge 51
Forbidden City, Beijing,
　China 59
Formeret 21, 31
Fortifications 18, 58
Fortified palace 59
Forum of Trajan, Rome,
　Italy 11
Foster, N. 54, 56
Foundation
　Ancient Roman
　　building 12
　Cathedral pier 15
　Modern building 54
　Nineteenth-century
　　building 50
Four-panelled door 47
Fourteenth century 26
　Arch 42
　Gothic building 23-25
　Medieval building 18-19
　Roof 44
　Style 22
Frame
　Door 46-47
　Medieval house 18
　Modern building 54
　Roof 16
　Steel 52
　Timber 14
　Window 48
Frame-construction walls 14
French baroque style 31,
　34, 59
French Flamboyant style 22
French Gothic style 58
French Renaissance
　style 59
French Romanesque
　style 58
Fret-pattern mosaic 42-43
Fretwork 9, 45
Friday Mosque of Ahmad
　Shah, Ahmadabad,
　India 59
Frieze
　Ancient Egyptian
　　building 7
　Ancient Greek building 9
　Ancient Roman building
　　11, 13
　Baroque church 31, 33
　Cathedral dome 41
　Cathedral pier 15
　French temple 39
　Medieval church 21
　Neoclassical building
　　30-31, 34
　Renaissance building 28
　Twentieth-century
　　building 53
Frog 14
Front door 47
Functionalism 54

G

Gable
　Gothic building 22-25
　Medieval building 19, 21
　Nineteenth-century
　　building 50-51
　Renaissance building 28
　Timber-frame house 14
Gable-and-valley roof 17
Gabled arch 23
Gallery
　Ancient Roman
　　building 13
　Baroque church 31-32

Cathedral dome 41
Medieval building
　18-20
Modern building 54-55
Renaissance theatre 29
Gambrel roof 44
Gangway 12
Gargoyle 25
Gate 19, 44-45
Gate-house 19
Gate of the Sun, Tiahuanaco,
　Bolivia 47
Gateway 8, 58
Gauged arch 50
Gentlemen's room 29
Gerberette 55
German-style baroque 34
Gilded band 44
Gilded cross 41
Gilded orb 41
Gilded rib 41
Gilt ironwork 34, 44
Girder 51
Glass 50, 52
Glass curtain 55
Glass mosaic 43
Glass pane 48, 52
Glass panel 46
Glass wall 54, 57
Glazed window 48-49
Glazing
　Modern building 54-57
　Twentieth-century
　　building 52
Glazing bar 48-49, 57
Glazing bead 46, 49
Globe Theatre, London,
　Britain 29
Glulam wall-plate 57
Glyph 8
Gopuram finial 45
Gothic architecture 20,
　22-25, 58-59
Gothic portal 47
Gothic stone arch 19
Gothic-style door 47
Gothic torus 22
Granite-aggregate slab 57
Granite cladding 52
Great Mosque, Cordoba,
　Spain 38
Great Wall of China 58
Greek-style fret ornament 35
Griffon 9
Grille 12
Groin 39
Groin vault 31, 38-39
Grotesque figure 28
Grundtvig Church,
　Copenhagen, Denmark 53
Gruppo Seven Cubist 53
Gryphon 9
Guilloche 37
Gujarati prayer-hall,
　Ahmadabad, India 59
Gutter 40, 50

H

Half-column 12, 20-21
Half-truss 16
Hall
　Asian building 45
　Hypostyle 6
　Medieval building 18-19
　Modern building 54, 57
　Neoclassical building 35
"Hall-keeps" 18
Hammer 39
Hammer-beam roof 22, 25
Hammer-post 25
Handle 47, 49
Handle-plate 48
Handrail
　Modern building 56
　Renaissance building 29
　Twentieth-century
　　building 52
Hanger 56
Harmika 45
Harmon, A.L. 52
Haunch 8
Hawksmoor, N. 30, 33
Head 48
Headers
　Brickwork 14, 39
　Nineteenth-century
　　building 50
　Tiled roof 17
Helicopter landing-pad 56

Hemispherical dome 29, 40-41, 44-45
Herring-bone pattern 42
Hieroglyphs 6-7
High altar 22
High tech style 59
High-tension beam 54
Himeji Castle, Himeji, Japan 44
Hinge 47, 48
Hip 53
Hipped roof 16-17, 28-29
Hip-rafter 16-17, 44
Hip-tile 17
Hispano-Maghrebi Islamic style 59
Historiated boss 21
Historiated keystone 21
Hittorff, J.I. 31
Hollow roll joint 17
Hong Kong and Shanghai Bank, Hong Kong 54, 56
Hood-mould 31, 33, 40
Hoover Factory, London, Britain 53
Horn 48
Horseshoe arch 38
Horsley Church, Derbyshire, Britain 25
Hotel des Invalides, Paris, France 49
House of Wonders, Zanzibar, Tanzania 59
Hti 44
Hypostyle hall 6-7
Hypaethral temple 8-9

I

Impost
    Ancient Roman building 13
    Cathedral dome 38
    Gothic building 25
    Islamic building 42
    Medieval building 18, 21
Inca building 59
Incline 20
Industrial Revolution 50
Inlay 42-43
Inner dome 15, 38
Inscription 42
Intercolumniation 9, 59
Intrados 21, 38, 48
Inverted ovolo 40
Ionic capital 8
    Baroque church 33
    French temple 39
    Renaissance building 28
Ionic column
    Baroque church 33
    French temple 39
    Neoclassical building 35
Ionic doorway 47
Ionic half-column 12
Ionic order 8
Iron 50
Iron railing 51
Iron roof 51
Iron shaft 48
Iron tracery 51
Ironwork 30, 34
Ish Khan Church, Tortum, Turkey 49
Islamic buildings 42-43, 58-59
Islamic mosaic 43
Italian Gothic style 59
Italian Renaissance style 59

J

Jacket-wall 18
Jack-rafter 16-17, 25
Jali 42-43
Jamb
    Ancient Roman temple 11
    Baroque church 31
    Medieval church 20
    Neoclassical building 30, 34-35
    Nineteenth-century building 50
Jami Masjid, Bijapur, India 42
Jettied joist 14

Jetty-plate 14
Joist 12, 14, 40
Jones, H. 51
Jones, I. 36

K

Kalasa finial 43
Kasugado Shrine of Enjoji, Nara, Japan 44
Kasuga-style roof 44
Kawana House, Japan 54
Keeled lesene 40
Keep 18
Kerb principal rafter 16
Keyhole escutcheon 47
Keystone 38
    Ancient Roman building 11, 13
    Baroque church 31, 33
    French temple 39
    Medieval church 21
    Neoclassical building 30, 34
    Renaissance building 28-29
King-post 25, 31
King-post roof truss 16
King strut 12
Knocker 47
Kondo of Horyuji, Nara, Japan 58
Krak des Chevaliers, Syria 58

L

Label mould 33
Lady Chapel, Salisbury Cathedral, Britain 22
Lamb-hinge 47
Lamb, T. 52
Lancet 23
Lancet arch 25, 38
Lancet window 14, 22-24
Landing 29
Lantern 40
    Baroque church 32-33
    French temple 39
    Neoclassical building 30-31
    Twentieth-century building 52
Latch 47, 48
Late Mogul style 59
Lath 12, 14, 17
Lattice-beam 54-55
Latticed screen 42-43
Latticed shade 53
Lattice-truss 57
Lattice window 50
Lattice-work 51
Laurentian Library, Florence, Italy 26-27
Lead came 48
Lead covering 16, 41
Lead roof 16-17
Lean-to roof 20-22, 24
Le Corbusier 52
Lemercier, J. 40
Lesbian leaf pattern 8
Lesene
    Ancient Roman building 10, 13
    Baroque church 32-33
    Dome 40
    French temple 39
    Gothic church 25
    Renaissance building 28-29
Letter-box 46-47
Library 35, 54
Lierne 21
Lift 55
Lift doorway 47
Light
    Renaissance building 26
    Twentieth-century building 53
    Window 48
Light-well 41
Limestone block 22
Limestone cladding 52
Limestone false door 7
Lintel 7, 52
Lintel course 35
Load-bearing wall 14

Lobby 56
Lock 47
Lock rail 47
Loft 29
London Bridge, Britain 18-19
Loophole
    Medieval building 18-21
    Renaissance building 29
Lotus flower 42
Lotus petal 43
Louvre 51, 56
Lozenge 23, 39
Lucarne window 32-33, 40
Lund Cathedral, Sweden 46-47
Lunette 15, 32
Lunette design 47

M

Machu Picchu, Peru 59
Madeleine, Paris, France 30
Maenianum summum 13
Mandapa 45
Mannerism 26
Mansard roof 44
MaODa
Marble-filled opening 41
Marble mosaic 43
Marble veneer 10
Margin 17
Martellange, E. 31
Mascaron 41
Mask 8, 37, 41
Masonry 14
    Ancient Roman building 13
    Cathedral dome 38
    Neoclassical building 34
Masonry apron 41
Mason's mark 22
Mason's tools 39
Mass-construction wall 14
Mass-produced brick 14
Mass-production 50
Matchboarded door 46-47
Mausoleum 59
Meander 9
Medallion 28
Medieval castles 18-19
Medieval churches 20-21
Medieval crusader style 58
Medieval houses 14, 18-19
Medieval wall ornament 14
Medinet Habu, Egypt 7
Merchants' Exchange, Philadelphia, USA 51, 59
Merlon 18
Metal construction style 59
Metal-frame wall 14
Metal-frame window 48
Metalling 40
Metal panel 54-55
Metope 8
Metric brick 14
Mexico City Cathedral, Mexico 59
Mezzanine 19, 54
Midway Gardens, Chicago, USA 53
Mihrab 42
Milan Cathedral, Italy 25, 59
Mill 10, 12, 50
Minaret 42-43
Ming Dynasty style 59
Moat 18-19
Modern buildings 54-57
Modillion
    Baroque church 31
    Ceiling panel 36
    Neoclassical building 30
    Renaissance building 27
Mogul style 59
Monolithic shaft 11
Monument 22
Moorish arch 38
Mortar 17
Mortise 46
Mortise-and-tenon joint 16
    Dome 40
    Door 46
    Nineteenth-century building 50
Mosaic 42-43
Mosque 38, 42
Mosque of Ahmad Shah, Ahmadabad, India 59
Mother-of-pearl mosaic 43
Motte 18

Mouchette 24
Moulded bracket 15, 38
Moulded corbel 51
Moulded stucco 36-37
Moulding 39
    Ancient Egyptian temple 6-7
    Asian building 44
    Baroque church 32-33
    Dome 40-41
    Door 46-47
    Gothic church 23-24
    Medieval building 18, 21
    Neoclassical building 31-32, 34
    Renaissance building 27-29
    Timber-framed house 14
    Victorian chimney 17
    Window 48
Mud daub 14
Mullion 48
    Cathedral pier 15
    Gothic church 22, 24-25
    Modern building 55-57
    Renaissance building 28
    Twentieth-century building 52
Multifoil 24
Multi-gabled roof 50
Muntin 46-47, 49
Music gallery 29

N

Naos
    Ancient Greek building 9
    Ancient Roman building 11
    French temple 39
Nave
    Ancient Egyptian temple 6-7
    Baroque church 31
    Cathedral dome 38
    Gothic church 22-25
    Medieval church 20-21
Neo-Babylonian style 58
Neo-Baroque style 50, 59
Neo-Byzantine style 50-51
Neoclassical style 30-35, 54
Neo-Gothic style 50-51
Neo-Greek style 50-51, 59
New State Paper Office, London, Britain 34
Niche
    Ancient Roman building 10
    Asian temple 45
    Baroque church 32
    Cathedral dome 41
    Cathedral pier 15
    Gothic church 23-24
    Islamic building 42
    Medieval building 19
    Neoclassical building 34
    Renaissance building 28
Nineteenth-century buildings 31, 34, 50-51, 52
Ninth-century building 44
Node 55
Nonesuch House, London Bridge, Britain 19
North Italian Romanesque style 58
Notre Dame de Paris, France 22, 25

O

Oak sill 48
Octafoil 23
Octahedral column 51
Octahedral dome 33
Octahedral shaft 51
Octahedral turret 23, 33, 51
Octastyle portico 10
Oculus
    Ancient Roman building 10-11
    Gothic church 24-25
    Medieval building 18, 21
    Neoclassical building 35
Oeil-de-boeuf window 48-49
    Baroque church 31, 33
    Cathedral dome 41
Ogee arch 42

Ogee-arched motif 44
Ogee brace 14
Ogee curve 24
Ogee-curved dome 40
Ogee-curved roof 43
Ogee moulding 27-29, 33
Ogee tracery 51
Onion dome 19, 40-42
Opera House, Paris, France 51, 59
Opera House, Sydney, Australia 54, 57, 59
Opisthodomos 9
Opus incertum 11, 13
Opus quadratum 13
Opus sectile mosaic 42-43
Orb 40
    Baroque church 32
    Cathedral dome 41
    Gothic church 23
    Neoclassical building 31
    Nineteenth-century building 51
    Renaissance building 29
Orchestra shell 53
Organ 22
Oriel window 14, 19
Ornament
    Asian building 45
    Baroque church 31, 33
    Cathedral dome 41
    Islamic building 42
    Neoclassical building 35
Ornamental arch plate 51
Ornamental metalwork 45
Ornamental panelling 29
Ornamental woodwork 19
Ornamentation 52, 58
Ornamented ceiling 36-37
Ottoman style 59
Outer dome 15
Oversailing fascia 29, 34, 40
Ovolo 40
Ovolo moulding
    Cathedral dome 41
    Gothic church 24
    Neoclassical building 32
    Window 48
Ovum 10
"Ox-eye" window 48-49
    Baroque church 31, 33
    Cathedral dome 41

P

Padmakosa 43
Pagoda 44
Painted roof 31
Paintings 42
Palace of Westminster, London, Britain 50-51
Palais de Fontainebleau, France 28
Palais de Versailles, France 34, 59
Palatine Chapel, Aix-la-Chapelle, France 38
Palau Güell, Barcelona, Spain 47
Palazzo Stanga, Cremona, Italy 34
Palazzo Strozzi, Florence, Italy 26-27
Paling 18, 29
Palmette
    Ancient Greek building 8-9
    Neoclassical building 31-32
Pane 48-49, 52
Panel 39
    Asian building 45
    Baroque church 31-33
    Cathedral dome 41
    Ceiling 36-37
    Door 46-47
    Gothic building 25
    Islamic building 42
    Medieval building 14, 18, 21
    Modern building 54-56
    Neoclassical building 30-31
    Nineteenth-century building 51
    Renaissance building 27
    Timber-framed house 14
    Twentieth-century building 52
Panelled door 46-47

Panelling 15, 29, 51
Panel moulding 46
Pantheon, Rome, Italy 10-11
Pantile 12, 34
Papyriform column 7
Paraboloid roof 54, 57
Parapet
    Ancient Roman building 13
    Asian building 45
    Baroque church 33
    Dome 40
    Gothic church 22-24
    Islamic tomb 43
    Medieval building 19
    Neoclassical building 30, 35
    Nineteenth-century building 51
    Twentieth-century building 52
Parapet rail 35
Parthenon, Athens, Greece 9, 58
Passageway
    Ancient Roman building 11, 13
    Asian building 45
    Cathedral dome 38
    Cathedral pier 15
    Medieval building 19
Passing brace 25
Patera
    Ceiling 36-37
    Neoclassical building 32
    Renaissance building 28
Paved floor 50
Pavilion 43, 53
Pavilion, Nara, Japan 58
Pavilion roof 17
Paving slab 29
Paxton, J. 50-51
Pazzi Chapel, Florence, Italy 27
Pedestal
    Ancient Roman building 10
    Baroque church 32-33
    Cathedral pier 15
    Dome 38, 40-41
    French temple 39
    Neoclassical building 31
    Renaissance building 28
Pediment
    Ancient Greek building 8
    Ancient Roman building 10-11
    Baroque church 32-33
    Neo-Baroque building 51
    Neoclassical building 30
    Renaissance building 28
Pendentive
    Baroque church 31
    Cathedral dome 38
    Cathedral pier 15
    Islamic mosque 42
Pentroof 44
Pepper-pot lantern 33
Perforated window 44-45
Peripteral temple 8-9
Peristyle 9
Perpend 14
Perpendicular-style tracery 24
Petal moulding 32
Piano nobile 26, 52
Piano, R. 54
Piazza 26
Pier 14-15, 38
    Ancient Egyptian temple 7
    Ancient Roman building 13
    Baroque church 32
    Gothic church 22
    Medieval building 19-21
    Renaissance building 28-29
    Twentieth-century building 52-53
Pier buttress 21-23, 40
Pietra dura inlay 43
Pilaster 14
    Ancient Greek building 9
    Ancient Roman building 11-13
    Asian temple 44-45
    Baroque church 31-33
    Cathedral dome 38, 41
    Cathedral pier 15
    Gothic church 23
    Neoclassical building 30, 35
    Renaissance building 28

Pilaster capital 35, 41
Pilaster-strip 33
Pile foundation 54
Pillar
  Asian buildings 44-45
  Domed roof 40
  Gothic church 24
  Renaissance building 29
Pilotis 52
Pin 17, 40
Pinhead 16
Pin joint 56-57
Pinnacle
  Baroque church 31, 33
  Gothic church 22, 24-25
  Medieval church 21
  Nineteenth-century
    building 51
  Renaissance building 28
Pinpoint 16
Pisa Cathedral, Pisa, Italy 58
Pitched roof 16
  Ancient Roman building
    10, 12
  Gothic church 23-24
  Medieval building 18-20
  Nineteenth-century
    building 50
  Renaissance building
    28-29
  Timber-framed house 14
  Twentieth-century
    building 53
Plain pilaster 32
Plan 9, 45
Plant capital 7
Plaster 36
  Ancient Roman building
    12-13
  Ceiling panels 36-37
  Timber-framed house 14
Platband 33
Plate 14, 51, 57
Platform
  Cathedral dome 41
  Medieval building 19-20
  Modern building 56
Platform stage 29
Plat lesene 32
Plaza 56
Plinth
  Baroque church 32
  French temple 39
  Islamic tomb 43
  Modern building 57
  Neoclassical building
    31, 35
  Renaissance building 28
  Twentieth-century
    building 52-53
Podium 11, 57
Pointed arch 18, 19, 21, 24
Polyhedral dome 40-41
Pompidou Centre Exhibition
  Hall, Paris, France 59
Popchu-Sa Temple, Popchu-
  Sa, South Korea 44
Porch 22-23
Portal 46-47
  Baroque church 32
  Renaissance building 28
Porta Nigra, Trier, Germany
  10, 13
Porthole 41
Portico
  Ancient Greek
    building 8-9
  Ancient Roman
    building 10-11
  Neoclassical building
    34-35
  Renaissance building 27
Post 33, 40, 48
Post-classical Mayan style 58
Post-modernism 54
Pot 16-17
Pradakshina 45
Prairie style 53
Preclassical Mesoamerican
  style 58
Principal rafter
  Ancient Roman mill 12
  Crown-post roof 16
  Dome 40
  Gothic building 25
  King-post roof truss 16
  Timber-framed house 14
Processional path 22
Pronaos 9
Propylaeum 8
Prostyle colonnade 35
Pseudo-Corinthian capital 28
Pteron 8-9, 11

Ptolemaic-Roman period 7
Pugin, A.W.N. 51
Pulley 48-49
Purlin 14, 16, 25
Putto 28
Pyramid 6
Pyramid of Cheops, Giza,
  Egypt 58
Pyramid of the Sun,
  Teotihuacan, Mexico 58

Q

Quadrant arch 20
Quadrilateral 43
Quadripartite vault 21
Quarrel 48
Quatrefoil 23-25
Queen-post 25
Queen-post roof truss 16
Quoin
  Baroque church 33
  Medieval building 18
  Nineteenth-century
    building 50
  Renaissance building 28

R

Rabbet 48
Radial wall 13
Radio mast 52
Raft 54
Rafter 16
  Ancient Roman mill 12
  Dome 40
  Gothic building 25
  Modern building 57
  Nineteenth-century
    building 50
  Tiled roof 17
  Timber-framed house 14
Rail 46
  Box sash-window 49
  Door 47
  Neoclassical building 35
  Timber-framed house 14
  Window 48
Railing
  Asian building 44-45
  Cathedral dome 41
  Medieval building 19
  Nineteenth-century
    building 51
  Renaissance theatre 29
Rainhill Asylum, Britain 47
Raking cornice
  Ancient Greek
    building 8-9
  Ancient Roman
    building 10-11
  Baroque church 32-33
  Neoclassical building 30
Ramp 19, 52
Rebate 48
Recessed arch 42
Rectangular pier 13, 19, 32
Rectangular window
  Ancient Roman
    building 13
  Asian building 44
  Baroque church 33
  Medieval building 18
  Renaissance building
    26, 28
Re-entrant angle 39
Re-entrant corner 31
Regula 9
Reims Cathedral, France 58
Reinforced concrete 52, 55
Reinforced plinth 57
Relief 6, 17
Relieving arch
  Ancient Roman
    building 10, 13
  Cathedral pier 15
  Medieval building 18-19
Renaissance buildings
  26-29, 59
Renaissance doorway 47
Reredos 22
Return 40-41, 48
Revivalist style 51-52
Rhombus 23
Rib
  Baroque church 31
  Dome 40-41

Medieval church 21
Modern building 57
Ribbon window 57
Rib vault 21, 38-39
  Gothic building 22
  Medieval building 19
  Renaissance building 29
Ridge
  Crown-post roof 16
  Gothic building 25
  King-post roof truss 16
  Modern building 57
  Nineteenth-century
    building 50
  Timber-framed house 14
  Twentieth-century
    building 53
Ridge and furrow glass
  roof-window 51
Ridge and furrow roof 50
Ridge-board 25
Ridge-rib 21, 39
Ridge tile 12, 28
Riley Church School,
  Britain 47
Riser 29
Robie House, Chicago,
  USA 53
Rocker-beam 54-55
Rococo style 30
Rogers, R. 54
Roller-blind 55
Roll joint 17
Roman architecture 10-13, 58
Romanesque portal 47
Romanesque style 20, 22, 58
Roman mill 12
Roman tile 17
Roof boss 20
Roofed space 31
Roofing tile 54
Roofless temple 8
Roofs 16-17, 38
  Ancient Egyptian
    temple 6-7
  Ancient Roman
    building 10
  Asian building 44
  Baroque church 33
  Dome 40
  Gothic building 22-25
  Hammer-beam 22, 25
  Islamic building 42-43
  Medieval building 19, 20
  Modern building 54-57
  Neoclassical building
    31, 35
  Nineteenth-century
    building 50
  Renaissance building
    28-29
  Twentieth-century
    building 52-53
Roof truss 16, 25
Rope and paterae
  decoration 7
Rosette
  Ceiling 36-37
  Neoclassical building 32
  Window 48
Rotunda 10-11, 34
Round arch
  Ancient Roman
    building 12-13
  Baroque church 31-32
  Cathedral pier 15
  Dome 38, 40-41
  Door 46
  French temple 39
  Gothic church 25
  Medieval building 19-21
  Nineteenth-century
    building 51
  Renaissance building
    26-27
Round-arched hollow 15
Round-arched window
  Ancient Roman
    building 13
  Baroque church 33
  Dome 40
  Medieval building 18
    20-21
  Neoclassical building 30
Royal Courts of Justice,
  London, Britain 48
Rubens, P.P. 36
Russian baroque style 59
Rustication
  Neoclassical building 31,
    34-35
  Renaissance building
    26-27

S

Sacristy 22
Saddle-bar 48
St. Basil's Cathedral,
  Russia 41
St. Paul's Cathedral, London,
  Britain 59
  Arch 38
  Baroque style 30, 32-33
  Dome 32, 40-41
  Old 22, 24
  Wall 14-15
Salient 18
Salisbury Cathedral, Britain
  22-23, 58
Sandstone 43
Sandstone brick 14
Sandstone tile 17
Santa Sophia Church,
  Istanbul, Turkey 58
Sash-cord 48-49
Sash-window 48-49
Saucer dome 40-41
  Ancient Roman
    building 10
  Cathedral pier 15
Scissor brace 25
Scotia 11, 35
Screen
  French baroque
    building 34
  Islamic building 42-43
  Twentieth-century
    building 52
Scrolled buttress 30
Scroll motif 22, 45, 47
Scroll moulding 18
Scroll ornament 28, 31, 39
Scroll-shaped corbel 34, 41
Scrollwork 24
Sculptural decoration 19
Sculpture 51, 53
Seating 13
Second-century building 10
Segmental arch 15, 50
Segmental head 48
Segmental pediment 10, 30
Selimiye Mosque, Edirne,
  Turkey 59
Semi-arch 22-23
Semicircular barrel vault 51
Semicircular tower 13
Semi-dome
  Cathedral dome 38
  Cathedral pier 15
  Islamic mosque 42
  Neoclassical building 34
Semi-elliptical arch 38
Service shaft 56
Set-back buttress 33
Seventeenth century 26
  Building 31-33, 42
  Capital 44
  Cathedral pier 15
  Ceiling 36
  Dome 40-41
  Roof 44
  Style 30
  Tomb 43
  Window 48
Seventh century
  Building 45
  Style 58
Shaft
  Ancient Egyptian
    column 7
  Ancient Greek temple 9
  Ancient Roman building
    11, 13
  Asian building 44-45
  French temple 39
  Medieval church
    20-21
  Modern building 56
  Neoclassical building
    30, 35
  Nineteenth-century
    building 51
  Window 48
Sheet-iron louvre 51
Shell 12, 28
Shoe 57
Shop stall 14
Shreve, R.H. 52
Shrine 44-45
Sickle motif 45
Side aisle
  Cathedral dome 38
  Cathedral pier 15
  Gothic church 24-25
  Medieval church 21

Side chapel 21-22, 31
Side entrance 33
Sill
  Ancient Roman mill 12
  Box sash-window 49
  Renaissance building 27
  Timber-framed
    house 14
  Twentieth-century
    building 52
  Window 48
Sixteenth century
  Building 28-29
  Ceiling 36-37
  Roof tile 17
  Staircase 24
  Style 10, 22
  Window 48
Sixth-century style 58
Skylight 51, 52
Skyscraper 52
Slab
  Ancient Egyptian
    building 6-7
  Modern building 57
  Twentieth-century
    building 52
Slate 16
Slate tile 17
Sloped turret-roof 17
Sloping roof 16, 40
Soane, J. 30, 34-35
Socket 16, 48
Socle
  Ancient Egyptian
    temple 6
  Baroque church 31
  Cathedral dome 41
  Cathedral pier 15
  Gothic church 24
  Medieval church 21
  Neoclassical building
    30-31
  Renaissance building 26
Soffit 12, 38, 56
Solarium 52
Solar panel 54
South American baroque
  style 59
South Asian buildings 44-45
South Italian Romanesque
  style 58
Span 38
Spandrel
  Ceiling panel 37
  Gothic church 23
  Islamic building 42-43
  Neoclassical building 34
  Nineteenth-century
    building 51
  Renaissance building 26
Spanish Renaissance style 59
Spiral scroll 46
Spiral staircase 24, 28
Spire
  Asian building 44-45
  Gothic church 22-23, 25
  Medieval building 18, 20
  Nineteenth-century
    building 51
  Renaissance building
    28-29
Splayed window-sill 27, 34
Springing point 38-39
  Cathedral dome 38
  Cathedral pier 15
  Crown-post 16
  Medieval building 19
Square 39
Square masonry 13
Square-panelled window 49
Square rib 40
Squinch 18
Staff 14
Staff-bead 49
Stage 29, 53
Stage-door 29
Stained glass 22, 48
Staircase
  Ancient Roman
    building 13
  Baroque church 33
  Gothic church 22, 24
  Medieval building 18
  Modern building 54-55, 57
  Neoclassical building 35
  Renaissance building
    26-29
  Timber-framed house 14
Staircase door 47
Staircase turret 20
Stairs 29
Stairway 43

Standing seam joint 17
Starling 19
Statue 24, 30
Statuette 28, 33
Stave 14
Stay 48
Steel 50
Steel and concrete floor 56
Steel-and-glass building 52
Steel brace 55
Steel casement-window 48
Steel column 55-56
Steel floor-plate 55
Steel lattice-beam 55
Steel-lattice mullion 55
Steel mullion 52
Steel-reinforced concrete 52
Steel roof 16
Steeple 23, 33
Stela 7
Stepped roof 33
Steps
  Medieval building 19
  Modern building 57
  Neoclassical building 35
  Twentieth-century
    building 53
Stile
  Box sash-window 49
  Door 46-47
  Window 48-49
Stilt 52
Stilted arch 20
Stoa 8
Stone 14
  Ancient Roman building
    11, 13
  Islamic building 42
Stone arch 19
Stone band 43
Stone block 33
Stone course 17
Stone foundation 50
Stone lintel 52
Stone panel 51
Stone plinth 53
Stone slab 6
Stone wall 33
Stone window 45
Strap-hinge 47
Stretcher
  Brickwork 14, 39
  Nineteenth-century
    building 50
  Tiled roof 17
Stretcher bond 14, 17
String course
  Ancient Roman
    building 13
  Cathedral dome 41
  Medieval building 18-19
  Nineteenth-century
    building 51
Strut
  Dome 38, 40
  Gothic building 25
  Neoclassical building 31
Stucco 36-37
Stud
  Ancient Roman mill 12
  Door 47
  Gothic building 25
  Timber-framed house 14
Studio Elvira, Munich,
  Germany 53
Study 29
Stupa 44-45
Stupa, Sanci, India 58
Stupica 45
Stylobate 8
Sumigi 44
Sun scoop 56
Sun-shade louvre 56

T

Tabernacle
  Ancient Roman
    building 11
  Renaissance building
    26, 28
Tablet flower 42, 45
Tack 17
Taenia 8
Taj Mahal, Agra, India 59
Tas-de-charge 21
Temple 38-39
  Ancient Egyptian 6
  Ancient Greek 8-9, 58
  Ancient Roman 10-11

(Temple continued)
Asian 44
Mayan 58
Temple of Amon-Re, Karnak, Egypt 6-7
Temple of Aphaia, Aegina, Greece 9
Temple of Athena Polias, Priene, Greece 8
Temple of Heaven, Beijing, China 44
Temple of Isis, Philae, Egypt 7
Temple of Mallikarjuna, Pattadakal, India 45
Temple of Neptune, Paestum, Italy 8-9
Temple of the Warriors, Chichén Itzá, Mexico 58
Temple of Vesta, Tivoli, Italy 11
Temple of Virupaksha, Pattadakal, India 44-45
Tendril 52, 37
Tenon 16, 46, 50
Tension brace 14
Tension-column 55
Tension member 57
Tenth century
Building 44, 49
Style 20
Terrace
Asian building 44-45
Modern building 55-57
Twentieth-century building 52-53
Tessellation 43
Tessera 43
Thatched roof 16, 17, 29
Third-century building 13
Thirteenth century
Building 19, 21-23
Style 22, 58
Threshold 11
Tie-beam
Ancient Roman mill 12
Crown-post roof 16
Dome 40
Gothic church 25
Neoclassical building 31
Timber-framed house 14
Tierceron 39
Tie-rod 50
Tile
Cladding 14, 17
Dome 40
Islamic mosque 42
Modern building 57
Neoclassical building 34
Renaissance building 28-29
Roof 16-17
Tiled roof 14, 17, 53

Timber 16, 36
Timber frame 14
Ancient Roman building 10, 12-13
Dome 40
Medieval building 18-19
Renaissance building 29
Walls 14
Window 48
Timber rafter 14, 16, 50
Toilet 35
Tomb
Ancient Egyptian 6-7
Islamic building 43
Tomb of Itimad-ud-daula, Agra, India 43
Tomb of King Tjetji, Giza, Egypt 7
Top-plate 12
Torus
Ancient Roman building 11
Dome 40
Gothic building 22
Medieval building 19-21
Torus moulding
Asian building 44
Dome 40
Medieval building 21
Renaissance building 27, 29
Tour de César, Provins, France 18
Tower
Ancient Roman building 13
Asian building 44-45
Clock 51
Gothic church 24
Islamic building 42
Medieval building 18-19, 20-21
Modern building 54-55
Nineteenth-century building 50-51
Renaissance building 28
Twentieth-century building 53
Tower Bridge, London, Britain 50-51
Tower vault 21
Tower window 49
Town Hall, Hilversum, Netherlands 53
Tracery
Gothic building 22-25
Nineteenth-century building 51
Window 48
Trachelion 8
Transept
Gothic church 22, 25
Medieval church 20-21

Transept facade 23-24
Transept roof 25
Transept wall 15
Transom 28, 48
Transverse arch 39
Baroque church 31
Medieval church 20-21
Transverse rib 39
Travertine shell 12
Tread 29
Treasury of Atreus, Mycenae, Greece 9
Trefoil
Gothic church 22-25
Nineteenth-century building 51
Trefoil arch 25, 38
Trellis window 7
Triangle mosaic 43
Triangular-arched doorway 47
Triangular buttress 15, 38
Triangular lesene 33
Triangular pediment 10
Tribune 19-20
Triforium 21
Triglyph 8
Trigon 42
Trimala 45
Trinity Chapel, Salisbury Cathedral, Britain 22
Truss
Gothic church 25
Modern building 55-57
Roof 16
T-section beam 50
Tudor arch 38, 47
Tudor-arched window 14
Tudor-style door 47
Tunnel vault 39
Turkish crescent finial 42
Turret 40
Baroque church 33
Gothic church 22-23
Medieval building 18, 20
Nineteenth-century building 51
Renaissance building 28-29
Tuscan capital 13
Tuscan pilaster 13, 35
Twelfth century
Building 18-19
Church 21, 25
Roof 44
Style 20, 22
Twentieth-century buildings 52-53
Twin-panelled door 47
Two-towered gate 19
Tyringham House, Buckinghamshire, Britain 35

U

Umbrella 45
Up-brace 16
Upper Belvedere, Vienna, Austria 34
Upper Frater, London, Britain 25
Urn 30, 33, 41
Utzon, J. 57

V

Valley-rafter 25
Vaulting shaft 20-21
Vaults 38-39, 54
Ancient Roman building 10-12
Baroque church 31
Gothic building 22
Medieval building 19-21
Modern building 54, 57
Nineteenth-century building 50-51
Renaissance building 29
Velarium 12
Veneer 10
Ventilation 10
Verge 12, 14, 50
Vermiculated rustication 34
Vertex 53
Vertical wall timber 14
Vessel
Baroque church 31
Gothic church 22
Medieval church 20-21
Vestibule
Ancient Greek temple 9
Baroque church 33
Medieval church 21
Neoclassical building 35
Victorian chimney 17
Victorian window 48
Villa, Godalming, Britain 47
Villa Rotunda, Vicenza, Italy 27
Villa Savoye, Poissy, France 52
Volute
Ancient Greek building 8-9
Baroque church 31, 33
Dome 40
Islamic building 42
Neoclassical building 30, 32
Renaissance building 28-29

Voussoir 38-39
Ancient Roman building 13
Neoclassical building 34
Renaissance building 26
Vyne, Hampshire, Britain 34

W

Wagon vault 39
Walkway 55
Wall-plate
Ancient Roman building 12
Crown-post roof 16
Tiled roof 17
Timber-framed house 14
Wall-post 12, 14, 17
Wall rib 31
Walls 14-15
Ancient Greek temple 9
Ancient Roman building 10, 13
Baroque building 30-31, 33
Concrete 54
Glass 54
Gothic church 22
Islamic building 42
Medieval building 18-19, 21
Modern building 56-57
Neoclassical building 31, 34
Nineteenth-century mill 50
Renaissance building 28-29
Twentieth-century building 52
Water-closet 35
Water-pipe 54, 55
Water storage tank 55
Wattle 14, 16
Wattle-and-daub
Ancient Roman building 10, 12-13
Medieval house 14, 18
Weathercock 40
Weathering
Gothic church 23-24
Medieval church 21
Renaissance building 29
Weather-vane 23, 29
Wedge 46
Weight 38, 48-49
Welt joint 17
Westminster Abbey, London, Britain 38
Westminster Cathedral, London, Britain 51

"Whispering Gallery" 15, 38
Whitehall Palace, London, Britain 36-37
Winding cornice 24
Windlass 19, 29
Window-frame 40, 48
Window jamb 31, 34, 35
Windows 48-49
Ancient Egyptian building 7
Ancient Roman building 11, 13
Asian building 44-45
Baroque church 31-33
Cathedral pier 14-15
Dome 40-41
Dormer 53
Gothic building 22-25
Medieval building 18-21
Modern building 56, 57
Neoclassical building 30, 34-35
Nineteenth-century building 50-51
Renaissance building 26, 28
Rococo style 34
Timber-framed house 14
Twentieth-century building 52-53
Window-sill
Baroque church 31
Box sash-window 49
Neoclassical building 34-35
Timber-framed house 14
Twentieth-century building 52
Window stage 29
Winter Palace, St. Petersburg, Russia 59
Withdrawing-room 35
Wooden panel 25, 46
Wooden roll joint 17
Wooden wall ornament 14
Woodwork 19
Wren, C. 30
Baroque church 32
Cathedral dome 38, 41
Cathedral pier 15
Wright, F. L. 53

X Y Z

Yasti 44, 45
Yellow marble mosaic 43
Ziggurat-style step-back 52
Zinc plating 29

Acknowledgments

Dorling Kindersley would like to thank:
Stephen Cutler for advice and text; Gavin Morgan of the Museum of London, London; Chris Zeuner of the Weald and Downland Museum, Singleton, Sussex; Alan Hills and James Putnam of the British Museum, London; Dr Simon Penn and Michael Thomas of the Avoncroft Museum of Buildings, Bromsgrove, Worcestershire; Christina Scull of Sir John Soane's Museum, London; Paul Kennedy and John Williamson of the London Door Company, London; Lou Davis of The Original Box Sash Window Company, Windsor; Goddard and Gibbs Studios Ltd., London, for access to stained glass windows; The Royal Courts of Justice, Strand, London; Charles Brooking and Peter Dalton for access to the doors and windows in the Charles Brooking Collection, University of Greenwich, Dartford, Kent; Clare O'Brien of the Shakespeare Globe Trust, Shakespeare's Globe Museum, Bear Gardens, Southwark, London; Ken Teague of the Horniman Museum, London; Canon Haliburton, Mike Payton, Ken Stones, and Anthony Webb of St. Paul's Cathedral, London; Roy Spring of Salisbury Cathedral; Reverend Gillean Craig of the Church of St. George in the East, London; the Science Museum, London; Dr Neil Bingham; Lin Kennedy of Historic

Royal Palaces; Katy Harris of Sir Norman Foster and Partners; Production Design, Thames Television plc, London, for supplying models; Dominique Reynier of Le Centre Georges Pompidou, Paris; Denis Roche of Le Musée National des Monuments Français, Paris; Franck Gioria and students at Les Compagnons du Devoir, Paris, for access to construction models; Frank Folliot of Le Musée Carnavalet, Paris; Dr Martina Harms of Hessische Landesmuseums, Darmstadt; Jefferson Chapman of the University of Tennessee, Knoxville, for access to the model of the Hypostyle Hall, Temple of Amon-Re; staff of the Palazzo Strozzi, Florence; staff of the Sydney Opera House, Sydney; staff of the Empire State Building, New York; Nick Jackson; Ann Terrell

Additional editorial assistance:
Edward Bunting, Mary Lindsay, Christine Murdock, Louise Tucker

Additional design assistance:
Alexandra Brown, Clare Shedden, Ellen Woodward

Additional photography:
Charles Brooks, Torla Evans, David Exton, Robert and Anthony Fretwell of Fretwell

Photography Ltd., Lynton Gardiner, Steve Gorton, Michelangelo Gratton of Vision, Peter Hayman, Nick Nicholls, David Rudkin

Additional illustration:
Roy Flooks

Research:
Vere Dodds, Danièle Guitton, Catherine O'Rourke, Vanessa Smith

Picture credits:
Page 7 false door stelas, page 7 plant capital, page 8 Doric capital, page 8 Ionic capital, page 8 Corinthian capital, page 43 marble tomb, all British Museum. Page 53 top: Frank Lloyd Wright, American, 1867-1959, Model of Midway Gardens, 1914, executed by Richard Tickner, mixed media, 1987, 41.9 x 81.3 x 76.2 cm, 1989.48. view 1. Photograph by Robert Hashimoto. Photography courtesy of the Art Institute of Chicago

Index:
Jane Parker